Buy and Wait: How to outperform, trade, and invest in the U.S. stock market

Copyright © 2018 Troy Bombardia

All rights reserved.

No part of this publication may be reproduced, stored in a retrieval system, or transmitted in any form or by any means, electronic, mechanical, photocopying, recording, scanning, or otherwise, except as permitted under Section 107 or 108 of the 1976 United States Copyright Act, without the prior written permission of the Author.

Table of Contents

1. What doesn't work   Page 5
2. What does work   Page 31
3. How to outperform with Buy and Wait. Step 1: Buy leveraged ETFs   Page 41
4. How to outperform with Buy and Wait. Step 2: Use fundamentals to help you avoid massive drawdowns during bear markets   Page 48
5. How to outperform with Buy and Wait. Step 3: Combine fundamental analysis with technical analysis to help you predict big declines in the stock market more accurately   Page 94
6. Closing Remarks   Page 108

If I told you that you can easily achieve 20%+ returns per year in the U.S. stock market through medium-long term trading, would you believe me?

If you don't, I have the data to prove it. I have built a [Medium-Long Term Model](#) that yields an average of 43% per year from 1950-present in the U.S. stock market. This Medium-Long Term Model is a quantitative trading model that doesn't require any discretionary input. The model makes all the BUY and SELL decisions. And the best part is that this model isn't complicated!

You can consistently outperform "buy and hold", the average professional trader, and the average professional hedge fund by combining fundamental and technical data into SIMPLE trading models.

In other words, "beating the market" in the long run isn't about having a 140 IQ or an economics PhD from Harvard. It's about:

1. Focusing on fact-based market instead of faith-based market analysis (looking at the data instead of believing in dogma).
2. Focusing on sensible instead of sensational analysis (focusing on the data instead of making buy and sell decisions based on the latest headlines).

Before I show you what works in the stock market, let me first explain what doesn't work. Knowing what NOT to do is just as important as knowing what to do.

What doesn't work

Here's a fact. The average hedge fund underperforms "buy and hold". The average professional trader does no better than "buy and hold".

Hedge funds that focus on U.S. equities returned half of the S&P 500's annual returns from 2009-2017, even though they charge lofty management and performance fees. Traders at banks are no better, which is why Wall Street firms have been consistently firing traders over the past 10 years.

*You can find the enlarged images in this book here https://bullmarkets.co/wp-content/uploads/2018/09/book-figure.pdf

Figure 1

Hedge fund legends are losing assets and underperforming
https://www.cnbc.com/.../hedge-fund-legends-are-losing-assets-and-underperforming.... ▼
Aug 1, 2017 - **Hedge fund** legends are losing **assets** and **underperforming** the market significantly this year. Tudor's BVI Global lost 1.9 percent year-to-date through July 21 compared with the S&P 500's 9 percent return in that time period, according to Bloomberg News. ... The fund returned 2.1 percent in July.

Underperforming super funds in the firing line – what it means
https://thenewdaily.com.au › Money › Your Super ▼
May 30, 2018 - But what exactly does it mean for a fund to be '**underperforming**'? ... and things like **hedge funds**, which are too complicated and weird to deal ...

Hedge funds: Overpriced, underperforming | Financial Times
https://www.ft.com/content/9bd1150e-1b76-11e6-b286-cddde55ca122 ▼
May 24, 2016 - It was the shot heard around the **hedge fund** world. After the New York City Employees' Retirement System decided to cash all its investments ...

99% of actively managed US equity funds underperform | Financial ...
https://www.ft.com/content/e139d940-977d-11e6-a1dc-bdf38d484582 ▼
Oct 23, 2016 - Almost all US, global and EM **funds** have failed to beat their benchmark since 2006.

The hedge-fund delusion that grips pension-fund managers ...
https://www.economist.com/.../the-hedge-fund-delusion-that-grips-pension-fund-man... ▼
Jan 18, 2018 - **HEDGE-FUND** managers may be feeling quietly smug about their ... Last year was the fifth in a row when **hedge funds underperformed** the ...

Hedge Funds Should Be Thriving Right Now. They Aren't. - The New ...
https://www.nytimes.com/2018/07/12/business/hedge-funds.html
Jul 12, 2018 - **Hedge funds**, on average, **underperformed** the Standard & Poor's 500-stock index yet again. An index of **hedge fund** performance, calculated ...

In other words, the average PROFESSIONAL in the financial industry does no better than the average mom-and-pop who does nothing except buy and hold stocks.

There is no other industry in the world in which the average nonprofessional is better than the average professional.

1. In the tech industry: the average professional programmer is better than the average person who is not a programmer.

2. In the plumbing industry: the average professional plumber is better than the average person who is not a plumber.
3. In the medical industry: the average doctor is more knowledgeable than the average person who isn't a medical practitioner.

But for some reason, in the financial industry, the average professional often underperforms the "shmuck" who buys and holds.

How can this be?

It's because standard trading strategies that are taught to traders and investors just don't work very well in the stock market. If you use standard trading strategies like traditional technical analysis, you probably won't be much better off than those who just buy and hold for the long term.

Most professional traders, investors, and fund managers make BUY and SELL decisions based on some key beliefs that are wrong. These beliefs cause them to underperform.

1. Professionals believe that more data is better than less data. They believe that successful trading is about finding esoteric data that nobody else has access to.

2. Professionals believe that complicated trading models and strategies are more successful than simple trading models and strategies. After all, how can you succeed and beat the markets with a simple strategy?
3. Professionals believe that you should focus on learning technical patterns, indicators, and many other seemingly advanced strategies that involve drawing a dozen lines on a chart. "The more complicated something is, the better it must be."
4. Professionals believe in their own strategy like a religion because they've staked their careers on it. To admit that their strategy is worse than buy and hold is to admit that their career has been a failure. Few people are willing to slap themselves in the face.

These 4 beliefs are all WRONG. Facts, data, and reality prove otherwise:

1. Simplicity is the ultimate sophistication. Using more esoteric data doesn't make you a better investor or trader. You will never find a holy grail that nobody else has access to.

2. Models that are more sophisticated aren't better. In fact, many highly sophisticated strategies and models underperform buy and hold!

A simple and logical strategy/model can easily beat most complex strategies by combining logical BUY and SELL signals with solid risk management. That's what the focus of this book is on. Using a lot of data and indicators doesn't make you a better trader. It just means that you don't know what's important and what's not important (i.e. you can't separate the signal from the noise).

3. A lot of technical analysis is just voodoo. Some traders spend hours every day on technical analysis and staring at charts, which doesn't really benefit their long-term performance. Much of it is just busy work – work for the sake of seeming "sophisticated". Traders who use insanely complicated technical analysis aren't much better than traders who use simple technical analysis.

4. Technical analysis is a secondary tool in the stock market – it is not as important as fundamental analysis. Technical analysis doesn't tell you WHY the market is going up or down right now. It just describes WHAT the market is doing right now and illustrates what MIGHT happen next. Fundamental analysis tells you what the market will PROBABLY do next.

5. Successful trading is about calculating the PROBABILITY of the market going up or down. Guessing what "might happen" is a waste of time. Anything "might happen". The world "might" end tomorrow. But if you consistently trade based upon low-probability events, you will underperform in the long term.

6. Most professional traders have a poor understanding of fundamentals. They focus on theory, dogma, and blind belief without studying the fundamental data in detail. Worse, a lot of traders begin with a market outlook and then cherry-pick the fundamental data to fit their view. This is confirmation bias at its worst.

7. Successful trading strategies are proved via historical backtesting based on data. In contrast, blindly believing in dogma leads to long term underperformance. For example, most traders believe that "rising interest rates is bearish for stocks". This is factually false. Historically, the stock market and interest rates tend to go up together.

8. Early = late = wrong. Predicting a market move too early doesn't mean that you're "smart". It means that you're wrong. A lot of "geniuses" constantly predict "the stock market will crash". But by the time their predictions come true, the stock market is still 2x higher than where they first began to predict that the stock market would crash.

For example, a lot of traders from 2009-present (2018) continue to predict that the stock market will "crash". These bears have been repeating the same thing from 2009 – present. The S&P 500 was at 1000 in 2010. Even if the stock market crashes 50% from the time of this writing (currently at 2800), it'll **still be 40% higher than where they first started to predict that the stock market would crash.**

Turning bearish too early is no different than turning bearish too late. Here's an example with the S&P 500 from 2007 – 2008. As you can see in the following chart, turning bearish too early means that you will sell before the stock market tops. Turning bearish too late means that you will sell after the stock market tops. As long as the SELL prices are the same, early = late. Being early doesn't make you a genius. You are no better off than someone who sells too late.

Figure 2

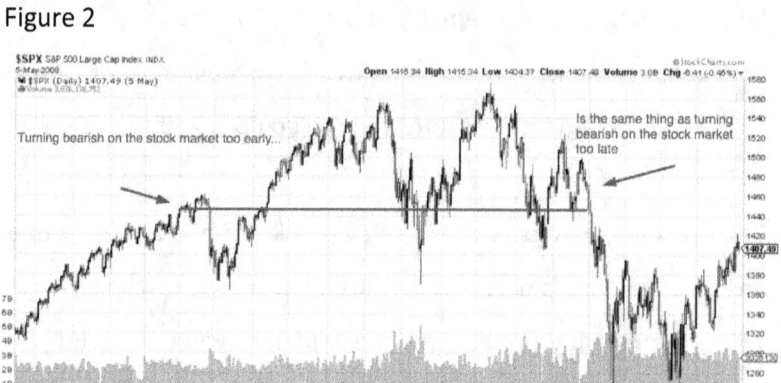

The opposite is also true when you're turning bullish. Turning bullish too early (i.e. trying to predict the market's bottom as it's falling) is no different than turning bullish too late (i.e. turning bullish after the bottom is already in). Here's an example with the S&P 500 from 2009. Early = late.

Figure 3

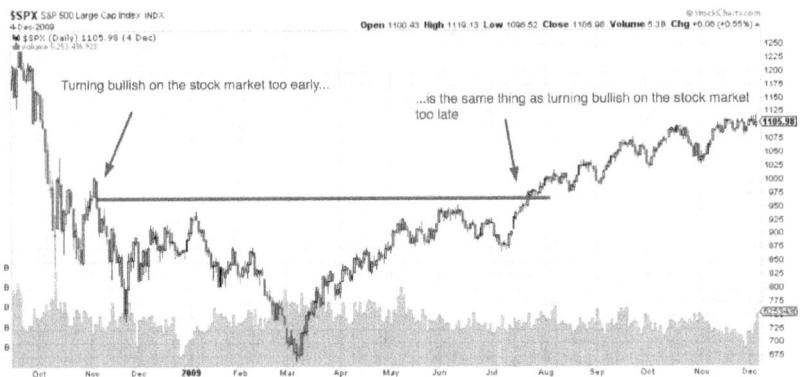

9. A high IQ is pretty much useless in trading and investing. If IQ mattered, professional hedge funds and banks would massively outperform. After all, these institutions are loaded with Ivy League graduates. In reality, these genius- staffed professional trading and investment firms UNDERPERFORM buy and hold. Successful trading and investing is about employing simple logic. It isn't about seeing who's the smartest one in the room.

10. Long term performance is more important than short term performance. This is a big reason why professionals underperform. Professional traders and hedge funds are taught to "always minimize your downside risk". They try to smooth out their returns and minimize their volatility through Sharpe ratios and other financial jargon. In essence, they are trying to achieve stock market-like returns (higher than normal gains) with bond market-like volatility (smaller than normal losses). That's not possible! By trying to minimize their volatility and

achieve a consistent 1-2% return per month, professional traders and hedge funds are killing their long term returns! It is almost impossible to achieve outsized long-term returns (e.g. >20% per year) without accepting periodic large drawdowns. The same concept applies to the business world. You will never have big wins if you can't accept a few big setbacks along the way.

Managing your risk to a certain extent is important. But you will kill your long-term performance if you put too much emphasis on risk management.

11. Fancy titles mean nothing in this industry. Lots of finance industry professionals like to tout their titles such as "I'm Chief Investment Officer of XYZ Capital". That means nothing in an industry in which the average professional can't even beat brain-dead strategies like buy and hold. Being Chief Investment Officer of a hedge fund that can't even beat buy and hold doesn't make you smart or a real "expert" in this field. It just means that you need to seriously re-evaluate your trading strategies.

12. "Geopolitical risks" are almost always overblown by financial media. Financial media loves to promote headlines such as "Geopolitical risk XYZ 'might' cause the stock market to fall". In reality, geopolitical risks almost always have a minimal impact on the stock market in the medium-long term. Geopolitical risks might cause some increased short

term volatility in the stock market, but they rarely have any long-lasting effects on the stock market. Moreover, financial media often flip-flops on geopolitical risks. For example, the day before Trump's election, CNBC was filled with headlines such as "the stock market will crash if Donald Trump wins the election". The day after Trump's election, every single headline was "the stock market will soar now that Donald Trump has won the election". Financial media is like airtime on TV. Something must be said, even during a dull day. Everything must be sensationalised, otherwise nobody would click on the news and watch ads.

Here's another example of financial media inventing reasons to explain the market's day-to-day and intraday fluctuations. In reality, most of the stock market's short term fluctuations are random. Trying to find a "reason" for these short term fluctuations is no better than random guessing.

Figure 4

BUSINESS NEWS   AUGUST 13, 2018 / 7:37 AM / UPDATED AN HOUR AGO

Tech gains push Wall St. higher, offsets Turkey currency worries

BUSINESS NEWS   AUGUST 13, 2018 / 7:37 AM / UPDATED AN HOUR AGO

S&P flat as tech boost offsets Turkish currency worries

BUSINESS NEWS   AUGUST 13, 2018 / 7:37 AM / UPDATED 39 MINUTES AGO

Wall St. slips as Turkey's currency worries hurt bank stocks

BUSINESS NEWS   AUGUST 13, 2018 / 7:27 AM / UPDATED 23 MINUTES AGO

Wall Street slides on Turkey currency shake-out

Reuters Staff   1 MIN READ

NEW YORK (Reuters) - U.S. stocks dropped on Monday as global jitters due to Turkey's plummeting currency spread to Wall Street.

The following chart demonstrates the most common "geopolitical risks" that didn't actually derail the bull market in the past 9 years. Listening to professional hedge fund managers and financial media would have been detrimental to your trading performance over the past 9 years.

Figure 5

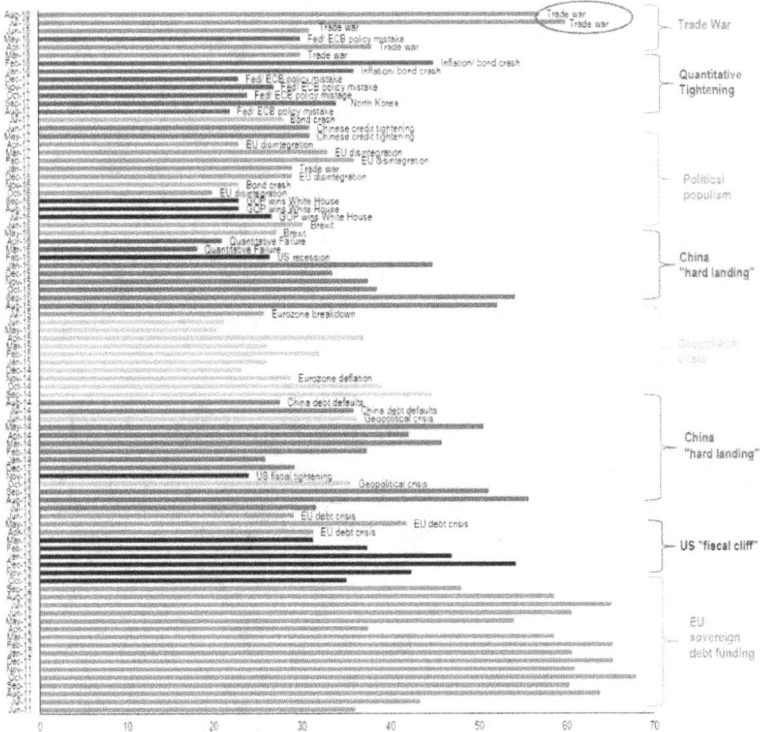

Exhibit 2: Evolution of Global FMS "biggest tail risk"

Source: BofA Merrill Lynch Global Fund Manager Survey

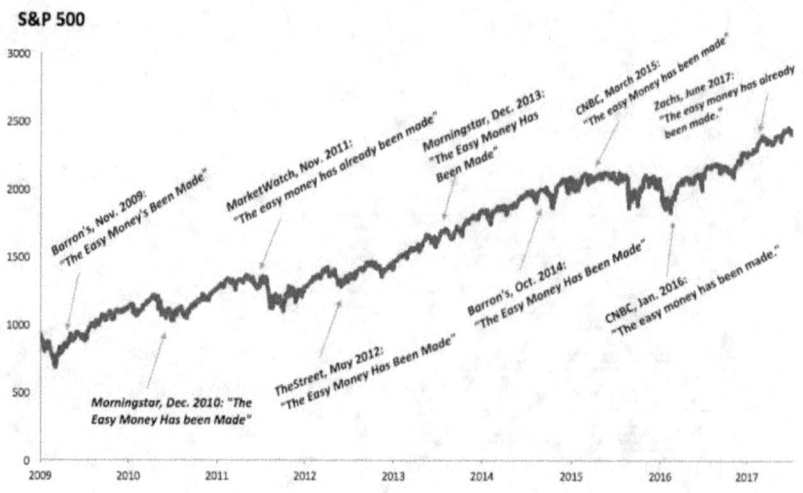

U.S. stock market traders and investors shouldn't worry too much about "contagion". The U.S. accounts for 43% of the world's total stock market cap (down from 50% in 2000). No country's financial markets come even close to the size of U.S. financial markets. To believe that a foreign country's economic crisis will cause economic and financial disaster in the U.S. is silly to say the least. In the world of finance, the U.S. is truly Goliath.

The average professional cannot even beat the average nonprofessional.

Some people argue that "not all hedge funds benchmark themselves to the S&P 500. Hence you can't blame them for not beating the S&P". While that may be true, think about it this way.

Buying and holding a S&P 500 index ETF (e.g. $SPY) is the easiest thing you can do. You can do it if you know NOTHING about trading and investing. Just buy it, forget it, and go to sleep. The purpose of investing and trading – no matter what market you trade or what your benchmark is – **is to make money**. If you're a hedge fund or professional trader who can barely beat the S&P in the long run, regardless of what market you trade, what you're really saying is:

I am spending 40+ hours a week in this industry as a professional, and I still can't beat people who do nothing.

What does that say about your strategy? You're wasting your time!

And let's not forget about taxes. Short term traders face a higher tax rate in most developed countries. Long term investors face a lower tax rate. So not only do professional traders need to beat brain-dead buy and hold, they must also beat brain-dead buy and hold by more than the additional tax burden!

If you're a professional trader who underperforms buy and hold, does this mean that you should give up on your career? No! It just means that you need to make some simple mindset adjustments that will get you on track to consistently beating your peers. A lot of what you've been taught is wrong. Once you unlearn the wrong things, you can start to learn the right things.

Why trading the stock market is the easiest game in town

Trading the stock market is much easier than trading other markets such as forex and commodities because the stock market has a long term one-way (bullish) bias. Other markets don't.

Figure 6

People who tell beginners to start by trading forex are usually brokers who want to generate more trading commissions. In reality, trading forex is much harder than trading the stock market. This is because currency pairs swing sideways over the long term. This is the U.S. Dollar Index. Notice how it swings sideways in the long term.

Figure 7

Since currency pairs swing sideways in the long term, the average trader will make **zero percent** trading currencies. Hence, any currency trader is fighting against zero. Remember probability distribution: the farther away you want to go from 0%, the harder it is. This means that e.g. only 5% of currency traders can average 10% per year, which is 10% away from the average of 0%.

The U.S. stock market is different. It goes up 7-8% per year (on average) in the long run. This means that the average trader/investor makes 7-8% per year in the stock market. Hence, any stock market trader isn't fighting against 0%. He's fighting against 7-8%. Remember probability distribution: the farther away you want to go from the average, the harder it is. 10% is a lot closer to 7-8% than it is to 0%. Hence, it's a lot easier to make 10% in the stock market than 10% in forex.

We looked at this concept in another way on the BullMarkets blog. We looked at the random probability of various markets going up on a 1 day, 1 week, 2 weeks, 1 month, 3 months, 6 months, and 1 year forward basis.

This is for the U.S. stock market

Figure 8

Probabiliy of the stock market being higher in...						
1 day	1 week	2 weeks	1 month	3 months	6 months	1 year
53.30%	56.50%	58.50%	61%	65.60%	69.60%	72.40%

This is for gold

Figure 9

Random probabiliy of gold being higher in...						
1 day	1 week	2 weeks	1 month	3 months	6 months	1 year
50.80%	52.50%	52.26%	51.67%	53.57%	57.07%	58.81%

This is for oil

Figure 10

Random probabiliy of oil being higher in...						
1 day	1 week	2 weeks	1 month	3 months	6 months	1 year
51.19%	52.90%	52.92%	53.50%	56.12%	54.41%	53.60%

This is for the U.S. Dollar

Figure 11

Random probabiliy of U.S. Dollar Index being higher in...						
1 day	1 week	2 weeks	1 month	3 months	6 months	1 year
50.31%	50.19%	50.30%	50.71%	49.01%	48.90%	52.40%

As you can see, the longer the time frame, the more likely it is for bullish investors in the stock market to make money. However, the probability of the currency and commodity markets going up vs. down is 50-50 on every single time frame. This suggests that there is more randomness in the commodities and currencies markets. Trading a market that has a high degree of randomness introduces an element of random gambling.

Speaking of gambling, here's a secret that successful traders and investors don't tell you.

TRADING IS GAMBLING. INVESTING IS GAMBLING.

However, there is a big difference between "blind gambling" and "calculated gambling". When I state that "trading is gambling", I'm referring to the idea that trading and investing is all about probability. There is no "sure thing" in the financial markets. There is no such thing as "the market will 100% guaranteed go up or down".

Hence, successful traders and investors use probability and expected outcomes to their advantage. Unsuccessful traders "guess" where the market will go next and generally have no systematic process in place.

This means that if you want to be a successful trader, you must predict what the market's **most likely direction** is.

Forget about "what could happen next". You see this on CNBC all the time: "this could happen", "that could happen". That's why the average professional underperforms buy and hold. They spend all of their time "worrying" about what "could happen next" that they ignore what will **most likely** happen next. If you're "worried" about something that "might" happen, stop "worrying". Do the quantitative studies to determine exactly how big of a concern something is. Stop guessing.

For example, Robert Shiller is a famous academic who predicted the housing bubble VERY EARLY in 2000. When the housing bubble burst in 2008 and housing prices collapsed, housing prices were no lower than when he first started to sound the alarm. Remember: early = late = wrong.

Figure 12

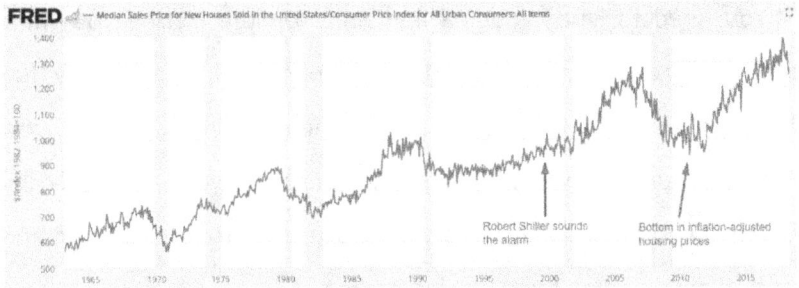

Robert Shiller sounded the alarm on the U.S. stock market in 2013. The U.S. stock market is MUCH HIGHER today than where it was in 2013. Even if the S&P 500 crashes 50% from where it is today (2800), it'll be no lower than where Robert Shiller first sounded the alarm.

Figure 13

ROBERT SHILLER: 'I Am Most Worried About The Boom In The US Stock Market'

In this book I will show you how to predict the U.S. stock market's most likely future direction using objective, non-"feelings" based trading strategies.

Ignore dogma and focus on the facts

You need to ignore dogma and focus on the facts if you want to consistently and accurately predict the market's most likely future direction. There's a lot of dogma in the financial industry that's wrong. People blindly believe in ideas just because everyone else is saying it. Too many unsuccessful traders and investors try to predict the market's **most likely** direction by relying on dogma.

For example, interest rates are rising at the time of this writing. That's why some investors think that the stock market "will crash". In other words, they're relying on the dogma: "rising interest rates are bearish for stocks."

And as usual, dogma is wrong. From a historical fact-based perspective: the stock market goes up more often than it goes down when interest rates rise. People who blindly believe in dogma are not able to consistently and accurately predict the market's most likely direction.

Some traders who don't employ probability-based trading say "this time might be different. The market might follow a low-probability direction today." This is true. The market doesn't always follow its most-probable path. This time might indeed "be different". But if you consistently trade against the most probable outcome, you will lose money or underperform in the long term.

So how do you test if a commonly accepted piece of "market wisdom" is true or useless dogma? Simple.

If a trading strategy or idea that financial professionals use **can't even beat brain dead buy and hold**, then the strategy or idea isn't worth the paper it's printed on.

All strategies, dogma, and ideas MUST be backtested and proven to be accurate with historical data. The future might not repeat the past, but if you don't use the past as a guide, you are literally "guessing" what will happen in the future. Traders who "guess" are not much different than blind gamblers in the markets. Dogma-based analysis is not much different than no analysis.

And lastly, do not use vague terms that have no predictive value. For example, financial professionals love to call something a "bubble", which is the catchall for "this market has gone up a lot, I hate it because I'm not making money on the long side, I don't really know when it will go down, but it will 'eventually' go down". A very common phrase you hear in the stock market is "this 'feels' just like 1999" (the year before the equity bull market topped in March 2000).

That's BS. Stop "feeling". Market analysis that's based on "feelings" = non-existent analysis. Let me tell you a secret: the stock market always "feels" like it's 1999 whenever it's going up. Stop trying to "feel" the market. Instead, try to estimate EXACTLY when the market will top or bottom. If you can't make **quantitative and precise predictions**, your "feelings" and "it's a bubble" warnings aren't worth 2 cents. Anyone can "feel" that the market will go down or "feel" that the market will go up.

Want proof that predicting the market's future direction via "feelings" doesn't work? A lot of people say "this market feels just like the runup to 1987". Except the market has "felt like" it's about to crash every single year, whereas it rarely does crash.

*For those who aren't aware, the U.S. stock market went up and then crashed in 1987.

Figure 14

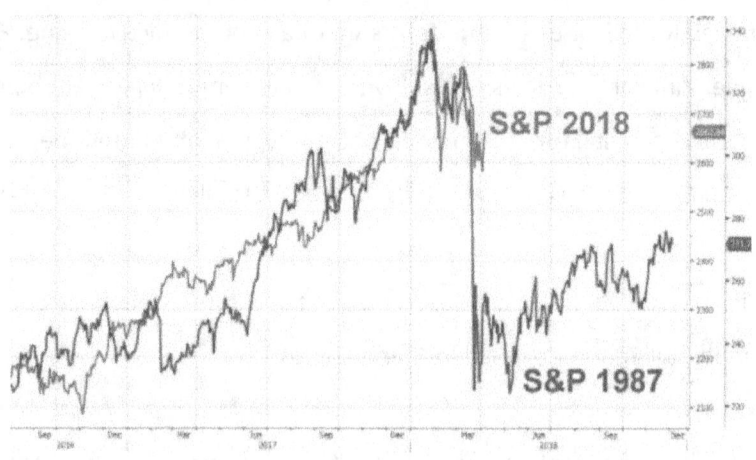

Figure 15

Figure 16

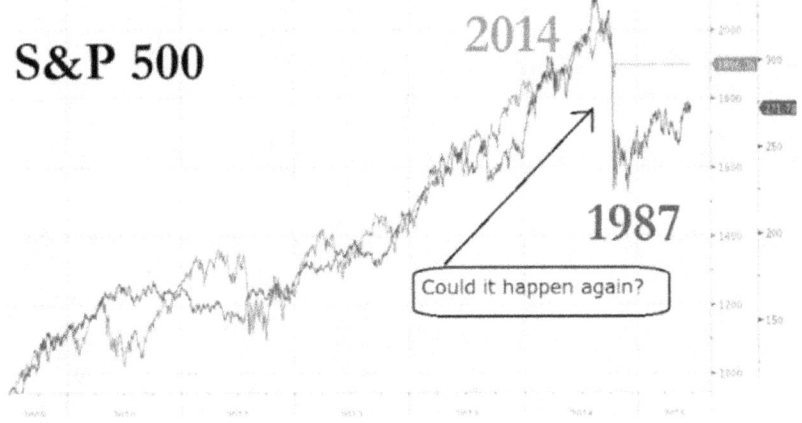

Stop "worrying" about what "might happen". Many professional traders and hedge funds underperform in the long term because they spend too much time "worrying" about bear market risks. Meanwhile, the vast majority of them aren't able to consistently and accurately avoid these bear markets (which I will demonstrate in this book). And if they have, it's at the expense of missing out on even more gains during bull markets. In reality, market crashes are rare, and they happen for **the same set of predictable reasons.**

What does work

"It was never my thinking that made the big money for me, it always was sitting" - Jesse Livermore.

Here's the bottom line. The easiest, most brain-dead thing to do is buy and hold. If your trading strategy can't even beat buy and hold in the long run, then what you're doing is a WASTE OF TIME. In other words, if more effort = less result, then you shouldn't be trading! Just buy and hold!

In addition, traders need to significantly beat buy and hold. Investors who do long term investing are taxed at lower rates than traders in most developed nations. So if you're a trader, then you must significantly outperform buy and hold to make up for the tax difference.

With that being said, you can easily and significantly beat buy and hold by using fundamental data and combining it with technical analysis. Outperforming in the long term is a simple process that I call "Buy and Wait". "Buy and Wait" has 3 steps:

1. Buy leveraged ETFs. The problem with leveraged ETFs is that they decay (erode) and lose a lot of value during bear markets.
2. Use fundamentals to help you avoid massive drawdowns during bear markets.

3. Combine technical analysis with fundamental analysis to give you more accurate BUY and SELL signals during bull markets and bear markets.

In other words, this simple "Buy and Wait" strategy states that you can significantly beat buy and hold by leveraging up during bull markets and predicting (avoiding) bear markets.

*I call this strategy "Buy and Wait" because practitioners buy and hold UNTIL the stock market is about to make a big decline. Practitioners buy and hold when the market is trending higher but sidestep massive declines in the stock market.

I'm going to show you how to use fundamental and economic analysis to predict the stock market's long term direction in this book. Fundamental and economic analysis is more useful than technical analysis, which has a LOT of false signals (e.g. fake head and shoulder patterns). A lot of technical analysis is just "reading the tea leaves". That's why many technicians underperform buy and hold.

Technical analysis on its own does not work very well. Technical analysis supplements and aids fundamental analysis. Don't believe me? Here's a simple fact. Most technical analysts are taught that "a break down below the 200 day moving average is bearish and a breakout above the 200 day moving average is bullish". This is factually incorrect.

If you go long the S&P 500 when it's above the 200 day moving average and shift into cash when the S&P 500 is below the 200 day moving average, you actually **underperform buy and hold**. Most technical indicators have too many false signals that hurt long term performance.

Figure 17

BullMarkets.co

Average annual return over the past 30 years if you…	
Buy and hold	8.09%
Go long only when the S&P is above its 200 daily moving average	6.56%

You can use economic data (fundamental analysis) to predict the stock market in 2 ways:

1. Discretionary method
2. Quantitative method

I will show you how to predict the stock market using both methods. But first, here's why the quantitative method is better.

Why you should trade using a quantitative method

Quantitative trading is better than discretionary trading.

What are quantitative trading strategies

Quantitative trading means that you build quantitative (data-driven) trading models to make your BUY and SELL decisions. These models are built by backtesting historical data and indicators.

In other words, quantitative models PROVE whether your trading strategy is successful or not through an objective, fact-based system built on historical data.

Why you should use a quantitative strategy

Discretionary traders are mostly just "guessing". For example, discretionary traders will say "chart pattern XYZ 'looks' bullish/bearish to me". They're basically just guessing where the market will go next without using data to prove their hypothesis.

Instead of guessing whether factor XYZ is bullish or bearish for the market, discretionary traders should quantify their ideas/factors and backtest them. "Backtesting" means that historically, did the market go up or down after factor XYZ appeared? If you can't quantify something, then you are blindly believing in it.

If you quantify an indicator or model, you can calculate EXACTLY how well it works based on historical data. You can calculate EXACTLY whether or not your strategy worked in the past.

Some people say "a quantitative trading strategy that worked in the past might not work in the future". Yes, anything "might" happen. But remember, probability is the key.

If you can't even use the past as a guide, then you have NOTHING to use as a guide. You might as well just guess and roll the dice. And here's the point some discretionary traders fail to understand. Historical analysis in the financial markets is important because ALL HUMANS make decisions based on things that happened in the past.

Here's a simple example. Why don't you touch the stove when it's red? Because when you were a toddler, you probably touched something hot and it hurt. You LEARNED from the past. You remember lessons from the past.

Why do discretionary technical traders use the 200 day moving average? Because people have used it in the past. People saw that when the market was below its 200 day moving average in the past, it was sometimes in a big bear market. So whether you realize it or not, EVERYONE is subconsciously using the past as a guide. They're using it as a guide to help them decide what to do in the future. Why are permabears afraid of "high levels of debt in the economy?" No one is born afraid of "high levels of debt". Permabears are afraid of this because in the past, high levels of debt have sometimes resulted in economic recessions. They learned from the past.

So instead of subconsciously learning from the past, you should consciously learn from the past and model the past using quantitative data.

Some discretionary traders don't like quantitative models and studies because "we live in unprecedented times – XYZ hasn't happened in the past". They're wrong. Same substance, just a different form. For example, when the internet came along, people said "we have no idea how this will impact the economy and stock market. We've never had the internet before." That may be true, but the internet is just another form of "a new innovation", which is the substance. There have been countless waves of "a new innovation" in the past, all of which merely took on different forms. The industrial revolution, electricity, cars, plastics, the internet, etc. A substance can take on many different forms, but usually results in the same thing. For example, new innovation (substance) usually results in economic growth and an equites bull market.

A more current example is how people commonly describe Quantitative Easing (QE) and Quantitative Tightening (QT) with the phrase "this has never happened before". People say "the Federal Reserve has never done QE and QT before". True, but QE and QT are merely forms of monetary easing and monetary tightening. The Fed has eased and tightened monetary policy many times in the past, and it has usually had similar effects on the economy and the stock market. Different forms, same substance, same result.

So now you know why trading with a quantitative model is better than placing discretionary trades. No matter what charts discretionary traders look at or how these discretionary traders "analyse" their charts, they are ultimately basing their decisions on "feelings" and guesswork if they don't incorporate quantitative analysis. Quantitative models take the guesswork out of trading.

You will be left with 1 of 3 results once you model your trading strategy:

1. The model/strategy worked poorly in the past. A strategy that worked well in the past might not work well in the future, but a

strategy that has consistently failed in the past has an even smaller chance of working well in the future.
2. The model/strategy has a mediocre track record. If a model/strategy is barely better than buy and hold, you are better off not wasting your time on this strategy and the "analysis" it requires.
3. The model/strategy worked consistently well in the past. You should use this trading model/strategy.

It's important to focus on building SIMPLE models. Simplicity is the ultimate sophistication. Using a billion indicators doesn't make you smarter – it just means that you don't know what you're doing. You don't know what's important and what isn't important.

The smartest people can explain VERY complicated concepts to a layman because they understand the ESSENCE of their topic, which is the most important insight. Just look at TED Talks, in which speakers present insanely smart and complicated concepts. But these accomplished experts always make the average person in the audience understand the topics being presented. They're able to focus on the key points: pick the signal from the noise.

Now let's go through the 3 steps in Buy and Wait, which lets you significantly beat buy and hold in the long term.

1. Buy leveraged ETFs.
2. Use fundamentals to avoid a big chunk of bear markets.
3. Combine technical analysis with fundamental analysis for more accurate BUY and SELL signals.

How to outperform with Buy and Wait. Step 1: Buy leveraged ETFs

What is a leveraged ETF

An ETF is a financial product that tries to match the performance of its underlying market. For example, the ETF $SPY tries to match the **day-to-day** changes in the S&P 500.

A leveraged ETF does the same thing as a non-leveraged ETF, except it **amplifies** the underlying market's day-to-day changes. For example, UPRO is a 3x leveraged ETF. It tries to match the S&P 500's day-to-day changes by 3x. So if the S&P falls -1%, UPRO will fall approximately -3%. If the S&P rises +1%, UPRO will rise approximately +3%.

Why buy leveraged ETFs for the S&P 500

The S&P goes up an average of 7-8% per year in the long term. By buying and holding a leveraged ETF, you **automatically outperform buy and hold in the long run**. If the S&P goes up an average of 7-8% per year, then buying and holding a 2x leveraged ETF like SSO or 3x leveraged ETF like UPRO means that you will **automatically earn more than 7-8% per year in the long run**. It's that easy!

The problem with buying and holding a leveraged ETF

Leveraged ETFs face a problem called "decay" (aka erosion). ETF decay occurs due to the mathematical nature of ETFs.

ETFs try to match the underlying market on a **day-to-day basis**. For example, UPRO seeks to match the S&P 500's daily percentage change by 3x. So if the S&P closes 1% lower than yesterday, UPRO tries to close 3% lower than yesterday.

UPRO does a good job at matching the S&P's daily percentage change by 3x. UPRO's decay/erosion comes from a long term mathematical issue.

Here's a chart of the S&P 500 since 1950.

Figure 18

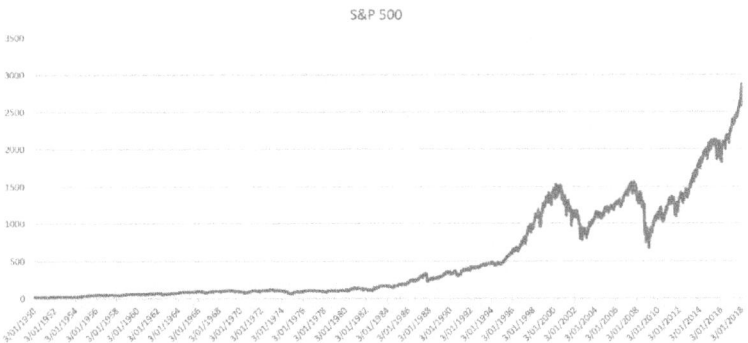

Here's a chart of theoretical UPRO (UPRO only began in 2009). This is calculated by multiplying the S&P 500's daily change by 3x.

Figure 19

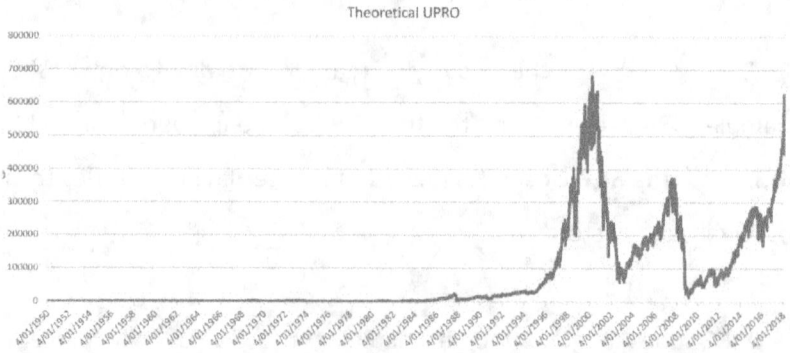

Notice 2 things:

1. The S&P's value in 2000 was almost the same as the S&P's value in 2007. Meanwhile, UPRO in 2007 was much lower than UPRO in 2000.
2. The S&P today is much higher than it was in 2000. UPRO is still lower today than it was in 2000.

The S&P has returned an average of 7.75 % per year from 1950-2017. Hypothetical UPRO has only returned an average of 16.38% per year from 1950-2017. As you can see, hypothetical UPRO hasn't exceeded the S&P's returns by 3x. It has exceeded the S&P's returns by less than 3x.

This ETF decay/erosion is caused by the way leveraged ETFs such as UPRO are calculated.

1. Leveraged ETFs match the underlying market's DAY-TO-DAY change by an amplified amount (i.e. 2x, 3x). They do not match the underlying market's (e.g. S&P 500) week-to-week, month-to-month, or year-to-year changes.
2. Hence, large declines in the underlying market cause decay/erosion in leveraged ETFs like UPRO. The larger the decline, the more severe the erosion. Bear markets (e.g. 40%+ declines in the S&P) account for the majority of UPRO's erosion.

Go to the BullMarkets.co website to learn more about ETF decay (erosion).

Decay (erosion) primarily happens when the market is going down. Here's a simple example.

Let's assume that the S&P falls -20% in one day. On that same day, a 3x leveraged ETF like UPRO will fall -60%. The S&P needs to go up +25% to get back to breakeven. If the S&P goes up +25%, UPRO will go up +75%. But 0.4 * 1.75 doesn't get UPRO back to breakeven! UPRO is still down -30% from its high! UPRO has lost value to decay/erosion.

As you can see, leveraged ETFs cause the ETF's **base number** to shrink. Multiplying a smaller base number is harder. E.g. if you lose 50%, you need to make 100% just to get back to breakeven. That's the asymmetry of losses vs. profits.

But on the positive side, leveraged ETFs also have COMPOUNDING. This is also due to the mathematical nature of ETFs.

Here's an example. Let's assume that the S&P goes up +10% today and +10% tomorrow. This means that the S&P will be up +21% at the end of these 2 days. A 3x leveraged ETF will go up more than 63%. It'll go up 69%. 1.3 * 1.3 = 1.69.

The more days the underlying market goes up, the more this compounding effect will occur. Strong rallies are EXTREMELY beneficial for leveraged ETFs because of the compounding effect.

To recap:

1. Investors who buy and hold leveraged ETFs will outperform investors who buy and hold without leverage.

2. But you must have balls of steel to buy and hold leveraged ETFs forever. Can you imagine buying and holding a leveraged ETF that has lost 90-95% of its value in a bear market? It would be a psychological roller coaster.

3. You can massively outperform buy and hold if you buy and hold leveraged ETFs only during bull markets. This is called Buy and Wait. In order to Buy and Wait, you must be able to consistently and accurately predict bear markets. More importantly, the amount of bear markets that you sidestep must exceed the amount of bull markets that you miss out on (because you'll probably sell too early). That's the problem with most traders. They put so much emphasis on avoiding downside that they miss out on too much of the upside. In the end, they are no better off than buy and hold.

How to outperform with Buy and Wait. Step 2: Use fundamentals to help you avoid massive drawdowns during bear markets

Everyone knows what technical analysis is. Moving averages, contrarian indicators, trend following indicators, etc. That stuff is all standard, and you can find it in any book. Here's an example of technical indicators for the S&P 500.

Figure 20

The problem with most traders is that they focus too much on technical analysis and not enough on fundamental analysis. A lot of technical analysis is just voodoo magic – reading the tea leaves. Many technical indicators are similar. For example, most contrarian momentum indicators are similar, so it doesn't make a big difference which one you use. Traders who spend too much time tweaking their technical analysis will only be able to make minor improvements to their trading performance.

Most traders focus on technical analysis because it's the easiest thing to do. Anyone can read lines on a chart like moving averages. Anyone can guess "the market 'should' go up because indicator XYZ is oversold".

Here's the reality: technical analysis alone is not much better than buy and hold.

Don't believe me? As we've demonstrated, using the 200 daily moving average as a BUY/SELL signal actually makes you underperform buy and hold, contrary to what conventional technical analysis tells you.

Figure 21

BullMarkets.co

Average annual return over the past 30 years if you…	
Buy and hold	8.09%
Go long only when the S&P is above its 200 daily moving average	6.56%

Do you know why most people don't use fundamental analysis?

1. Because it's hard. Anyone can read lines on a chart, even if most of those lines don't mean anything. Contrary to what some technical analysts think, the market doesn't want to go "touch" a trendline. The market doesn't have a brain. It's an inanimate object.
2. Most traders "guess" what the fundamentals mean for the stock market. This leaves them frustrated and confused when e.g. the stock market goes up on a "weak" Jobs Report.

Most people "guess" what the fundamentals are. "I think rising interest rates are bad for the economy, because that's what other people are saying, my economics professors taught me in university, etc".

Most people don't use a SYSTEMATIC approach to understanding fundamentals. Or worse, some traders cherry-pick the fundamental data to fit their pre-determined view of the world. They confuse the noise for the signal.

1. For example, they look at one piece of bad economic data and conclude that "the economy is doomed", regardless of what the rest of the data suggests.

2. For example, they look at one piece of good economic data and conclude that "the economy is solid", regardless of what the rest of the data suggests.

In reality, there will always be bad fundamental data, even in the best of times. There will always be good fundamental data, even in the worst of times. The world will never be 100% perfect or 100% terrible. Permabears ALWAYS point to the bad fundamentals, even when most of the fundamentals are good. Permabulls ALWAYS point to the good fundamentals, even when most of the fundamentals are bad.

*Permabears are investors/traders who are always bearish on the market, regardless of the facts. They are diehard bears.
*Permabulls are investors/traders who are always bullish on the market, regardless of the facts. They are diehard bulls.

Hence, what matters is whether the MAJORITY of the IMPORTANT economic indicators are improving or deteriorating. Look at the forest. Ignore the trees. This is the key to fundamental analysis for the stock market.

The economy and stock market move in the same direction in the medium-long term

This is a very simple and logical concept that most traders don't seem to understand because they focus on the trees (small picture) instead of the forest (big picture). Separating the signal from the noise is all about focusing on the big picture.

The economy and stock market move in the same direction in the medium-long term. Sounds logical, doesn't it? Why is this?

To understand this phenomenon, we need to understand what a stock is. A stock represents ownership in a company. The owner of that stock owns a part of the company's ability to earn PROFITS.

1. People are willing to pay more for a company that makes more profits, hence they bid up the stock price.
2. People are willing to pay less for a company that makes less profits, hence they bid down the stock price.

For any individual company, its profits are the result of its competitiveness in the marketplace. But what about profits for the corporate sector as a whole? What drives profits for all of Corporate America? The economy. The stock market's fundamentals = the U.S. economy.

If the economy improves, consumers and businesses will be more willing to spend, so corporate profits will go up. If the economy deteriorates, consumers and businesses will be less willing to spend, so corporate profits will go down.

That's why good stock market traders and investors should focus on the state of the economy. An improving economy = higher corporate profits for Corporate America as a whole = bullish for the stock market in the long term.

A deteriorating economy = lower corporate profits for Corporate America = bearish for the stock market in the long term.

Here's proof that the U.S. stock market and the U.S. economy move in the same direction in the medium-long term. This is a chart of the S&P 500 from 1950-present, using a log scale.

Figure 22

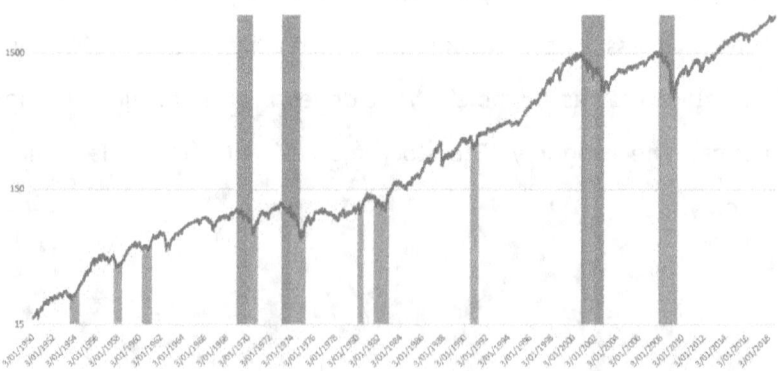

Grey represents economic recessions and orange represents the S&P 500's "bear markets" in the above chart.

*My Medium-Long Term Model defines "bear markets" as 40%+ declines that last 1 year or more. I don't arbitrarily define "bear markets" as 20%+ declines. In reality, 20% declines are no different from 19% declines or 18% declines. For my Medium-Long Term Model, 20% declines are "big corrections".

As you can see in the chart above, all bear markets occur in the context of economic recessions. Recessions that don't lead to bear markets often lead to "big corrections" in the stock market. So in order for the stock market to enter into a bear market, the economy must show symptoms that it's about to enter into a recession.

Bear markets start before economic recessions begin. There have been 4 bear markets from 1950-present.

1. October 11, 2007 – March 6, 2009. The recession began in December 2007, 2 months after the bear market began.
2. September 1, 2000 – October 10, 2002. The recession began in March 2001, 6 months after the bear market began.
3. January 11, 1973 – October 4, 1974. The recession began in November 1973, 10 months after the bear market began.

4. December 2, 1968 – May 26, 1970. The recession began in December 1969, 1 year after the bear market began.

Since bear markets begin before economic recessions begin, we need to focus on LEADING economic indicators. Leading economic indicators deteriorate BEFORE recessions begin. Hence, leading economic indicators can predict the stock market's bull-bear transitions in a timelier manner. I will show you how these leading economic indicators predict the stock market's bull-bear transitions later in this book.

It's important to focus on the OVERALL TREND in the economic data. Bad traders lose themselves in the data's meaningless month-to-month fluctuations. The reality is that the economy is never going to improve nonstop. The economy is never going to deteriorate nonstop. What matters is the trend. Remember to focus on the forest and not the trees. There will be always small problems from time to time. But as long as the overall trend is improving, then the economy is improving. Focus on the data as a whole.

Short term fluctuations in the economic data don't matter because a lot of it is just meaningless randomness. Every single economic statistic has some statistical randomness to it, which means that any single month's reading might be inaccurate. Also, it is normal for the economy to take a small step back every once in a while. It doesn't mean that all hell will break loose. Think of it this way. Let's assume that you're in business and you gained 10 clients but then lost 1 client. Does losing 1 client mean that you had a bad month? Of course not! You still gained 9 clients! Focus on the forest instead of the trees.

Valuations don't matter

One of the biggest mistakes traders and investors make is to focus excessively on valuations. They think a market that's overvalued "must" go down and a market that's undervalued "must" go up.

*According to financial dogma, a market that's "overvalued" is "too expensive" and a market that's "undervalued" is "too cheap".

This is factually false. For example, the stock market has been CONSISTENTLY overvalued from 1995-present. Anyone who got out of stocks in 1995 just because it was "overvalued" would have missed out on massive gains.

The following chart demonstrates Tobin's Q Ratio, a popular valuation indicator for the U.S. stock market. The stock market is "overvalued" when the Q Ratio is above its long term average (0.7) and "undervalued" when the Q Ratio is below its long term average (0.7). As you can see, the stock market has been consistently overvalued from 1995-present.

Figure 23

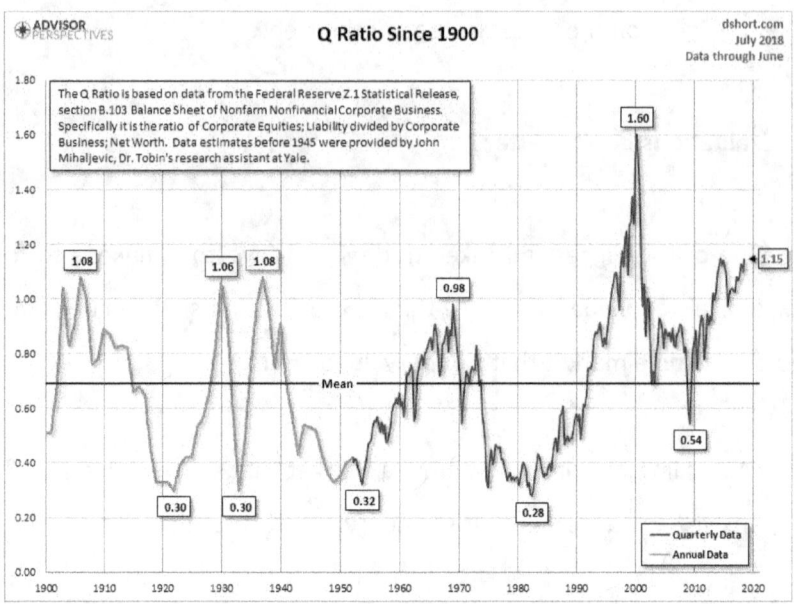

The following chart demonstrates the Corporate Equities to GDP Ratio, another popular valuation indicator for the U.S. stock market. The stock market is "overvalued" when this ratio is high and "undervalued" when this ratio is low. As you can see, this ratio has been consistently high (overvalued) in the past 20 years.

Figure 24

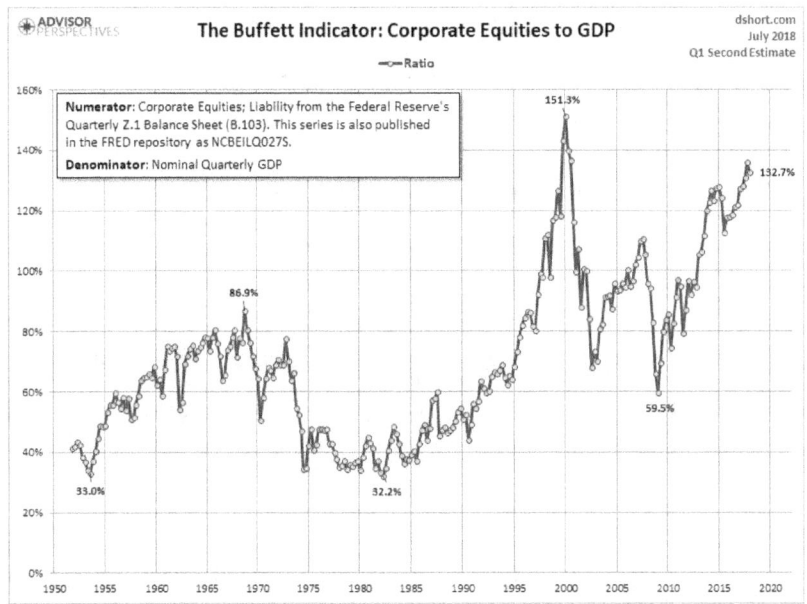

Valuations tell us where the market will go in the next 5-10 years. It doesn't tell us where the market will go in the near future (i.e. next 1-2 years).

1. If valuations are "high" (overvalued) right now, the stock market will probably be lower in 5-10 years. But it doesn't tell us where the stock market will go in the interim.
2. If valuations are "low (undervalued) right now, the stock market will probably be higher in 5-10 years. But it doesn't tell us where the stock market will go in the interim.

So unless your trading time frame is 5-10 years, you should not pay too much attention to valuations when making buy and sell decisions.

Focus on the U.S. economy when trading the U.S. stock market. Downplay the importance of the global economy.

But what about the global economy? Don't we live in an increasingly interconnected global economy? Shouldn't U.S. stock market traders also focus on what's going on outside the U.S.?

Yes, it's true that we live in an interconnected global economy. Around 50% of the S&P 500's corporate revenues and earnings come from overseas sources. But more importantly, the U.S. economy is the world's most DYNAMIC economy (i.e. the U.S. economy leads the global economy). This means that:

1. The U.S. will deteriorate first in a truly global recession. This means that the U.S. economy leads both global economic expansions and recessions. For example, the global economy only deteriorated in 2008, AFTER the U.S. economy had deteriorated in 2007.
2. Sometimes there will be periodic regional weakness. For example, emerging market economies deteriorated from 2011-2016, but that did not affect the U.S. economy. Those foreign economies won't crater as long as the U.S. economy doesn't

crater. They'll experience a small recession/economic downturn, but because the U.S. economy doesn't go down, they won't go down too much either. Eventually they'll go up with the U.S. economy.

This means that the U.S. economy leads the global economy during big turning points in the global economy such as the 2007 economic expansion top and the 2009 recession's bottom. Meanwhile, the U.S. economy mostly shrugs off the impact of foreign economic weakness because the U.S. is a relatively isolated economy.

Figure 25

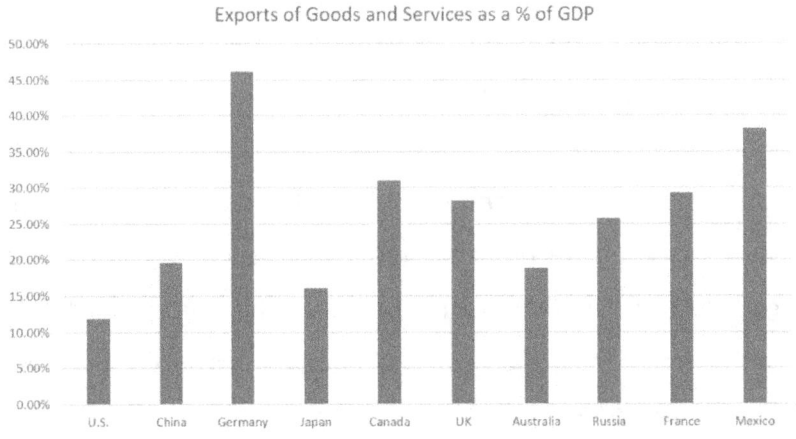

What is "fundamental analysis" for the stock market

Too many people spend their time trying to "predict" what will happen next. Worse, they try to predict far into the future. In reality, these distant predictions are a waste of time.

NOBODY can consistently and accurately predict far into the future. Just look at the "geniuses" who predicted the last crash. How many wrong predictions have they made? When you toss out 10 different predictions, one of them will become a reality. But as a batting average, most of these guys are no better than random. 1 successful prediction and 9 failed predictions = a 10% accuracy rate.

But here's the beauty about fundamental analysis for the stock market. You don't need to "predict" what will happen next. You only need to know what's happening right now. If you know how to read, you will know what the stock market will most likely do next.

But wait a second, didn't everyone tell you that "the stock market usually peaks before economic recessions begin? Isn't a recession a lagging indicator for the stock market"? Yes. That is true. HOWEVER, not all economic indicators are equal. A "recession" is only deemed by one indicator – GDP. GDP is a lagging indicator. You need to use leading economic indicators. The economy and stock market move in the same direction in the medium-long term. Hence, a leading indicator for the economy is also a leading indicator for the stock market.

Once again, here's another chart of the S&P 500 from 1950-present with recessions shaded in grey. Notice how almost all of the massive stock market declines occur within the context of economic recessions.

Figure 26

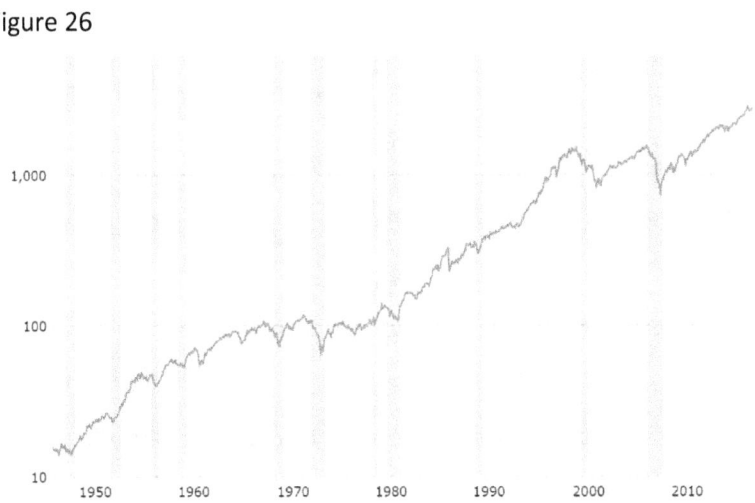

The following is the Wilshire 5000's chart. The Wilshire 5000 encompasses the entire U.S. stock market while the S&P 500 encompasses 80% of the U.S. stock market. Like the S&P 500, the Wilshire 5000 almost only makes major declines when the economy sinks into a recession.

Figure 27

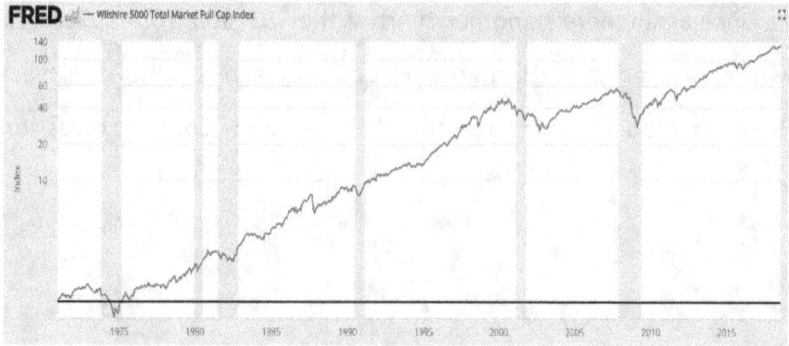

The order of events usually looks like this. At the stock market's tops:

1. Leading economic indicators deteriorate first.
2. The stock market tops.
3. GDP tops, a recession begins, and corporate earnings go down.

At bear market bottoms, things are a little different:

1. The stock market bounces. The first rally of a new bull market is usually an oversold rally, just like any standard rally in a bear market.
2. Then the economy improves. That turns the bear market rally into the first leg of a bull market, so the rally continues.

Now I'm going to show you which leading economic indicators you should monitor on a regular basis. Remember, focus on the overall trend in these economic indicators.

Leading indicators for the stock market and economy

The stock market and economy move in the same direction in the medium-long term. Hence, a leading indicator for the economy is also a leading indicator for the stock market. In this part of the book we're going to look at these leading indicators.

When looking at leading indicators, you should find leading indicators that are TIMELY and CONSISTENT. Here's what this means.

A "TIMELY" leading indicator leads the stock market, but not by too much. Some leading indicators lead the stock market by too much, which gives you a bearish signal too early. Remember, early = late = wrong. If you turn bearish and sell too early, you will miss out on too much of the stock market's rally. This means that you can potentially underperform buy and hold.

Housing Starts is an example of a leading indicator that's TOO early. Housing Starts can start to trend downwards YEARS before an economic recession or bear market begins.

Figure 27

*Recession = grey areas

And of course, lagging economic indicators aren't useful. GDP already lags the stock market. If you find an economic indicator that lags GDP, then you will lag the stock market even more. You will turn bearish and SELL very, very late.

For example, Retail Sales is a lagging indicator. Year-over-year Retail Sales growth turns negative AFTER recessions have already begun.

Figure 28

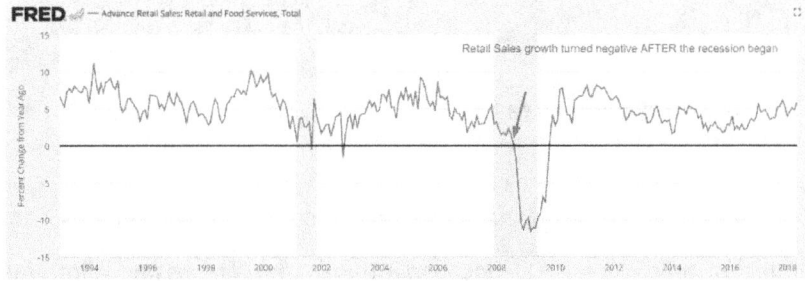

*Recession = grey areas

A "CONSISTENT" leading indicator means 3 things.

1. A "consistent" indicator does not give you too many false positives. Some "leading indicators" are pretty useless. They have successfully predicted some recessions, but they also predict a lot of "recessions" that don't actually happen.

This is an example featuring the manufacturing section of Industrial Production. Notice how the economy doesn't always slip into a recession when the year-over-year Industrial Production growth turns negative.

Figure 29

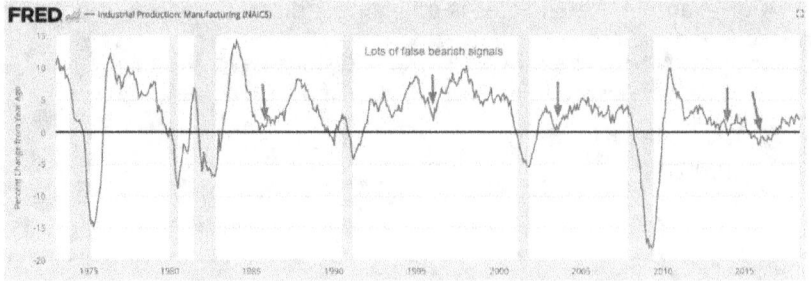

*Recession = grey areas

These failed SELL signals are problematic. If the failed economic indicator tells you to SELL because it thinks that a recession is imminent, but a recession doesn't actually materialize, you will be on the sidelines while the stock market rallies higher. You will need to buy your stocks back at much higher prices. In other words, you underperformed buy and hold.

2. A "consistent" indicator should not fail to predict a recession that actually materializes.

In other words, you should focus on leading economic indicators that closely approximate the tops before ALL bear markets and economic recessions begin but don't give you too many false positives. No more, no less.

In addition, indicators with more historical data (that go further back in history) are better than indicators with less historical data. An indicator may seem perfect, but if it doesn't have enough historical data, you don't know where its flaws are.

3. A "consistent" indicator should "lead" by a pretty consistent amount of TIME.

Some indicators will lead by a very wide range in terms of TIME. For example, sometimes Leading Indicator XYZ will start to deteriorate 3 years before the stock market tops, and sometimes Leading Indicator XYZ will start to deteriorate 1 year before the stock market tops. This is problematic because you must be consistent when deciding how to use an indicator. You can't decide "sometimes I'll turn bearish when

Indicator XYZ deteriorates for 6 months, sometimes I'll turn bearish when Indicator XYZ deteriorates for 3 years". You must be consistent and decide "I'll turn bearish whenever Indicator XYZ deteriorates for X months". If an indicator "leads" by a wildly fluctuating amount of TIME, sometimes you will turn bearish too early.

With that being said, here is a list of leading economic indicators that you should monitor on a regular basis. You can find my current analysis of these economic indicators on my blog.

Useful leading economic indicators

Unemployment Rate

The Unemployment Rate is the percentage of people who are looking for work but are unemployed.

The Unemployment Rate is a timely and consistent leading economic indicator. It tends to trend upwards just before a bear market and recession begins.

Figure 30

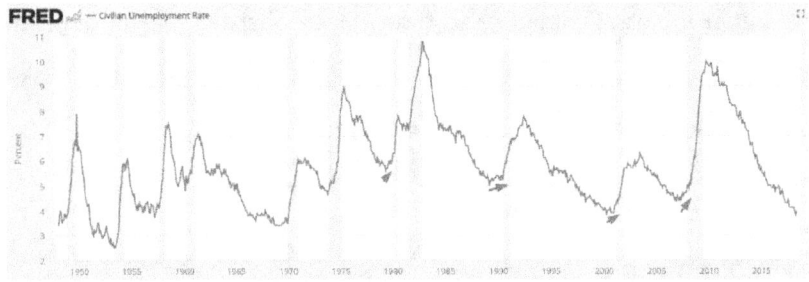

*Grey = recessions

Figure 31

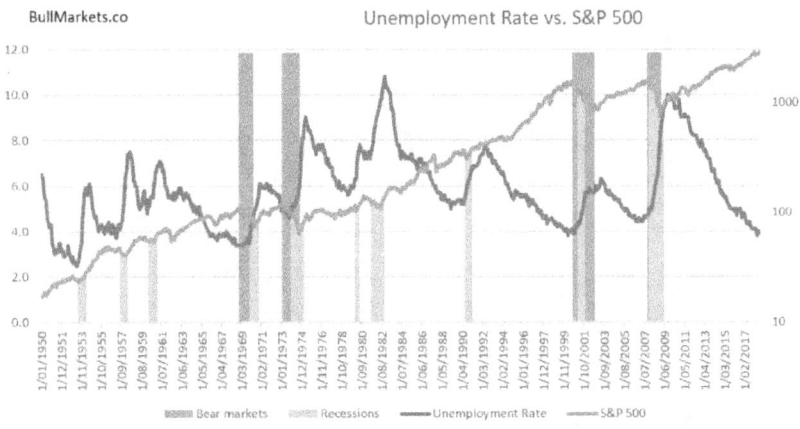

Initial Jobless Claims

Initial Jobless Claims measures the number of jobless claims filed by people who are seeking to receive jobless benefits. In other words, this measures the number of people who are recently unemployed.

Initial Jobless Claims is also timely and consistent. It tends to trend upwards a little earlier than the Unemployment Rate, which makes it slightly more useful than the Unemployment Rate.

Figure 32

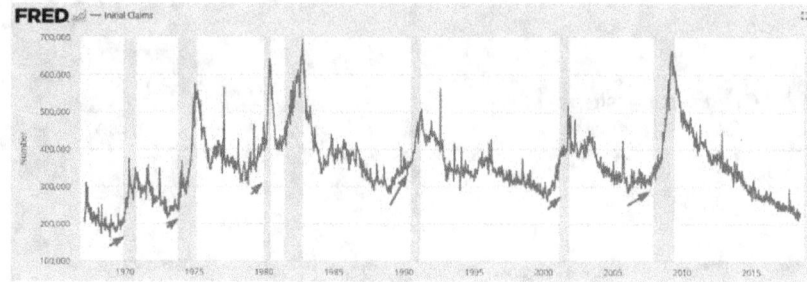

Figure 33

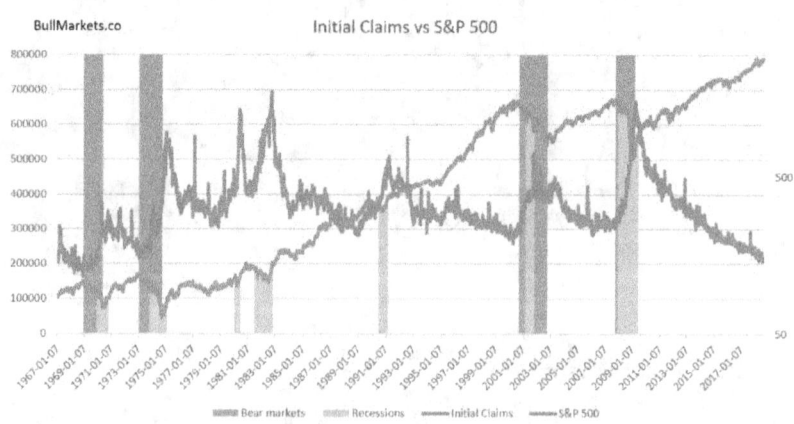

KC Fed Labor Markets Index

The Kansas City Fed produces a Labor Markets Index. Similar to the Unemployment Rate and Initial Claims, the Labor Markets Index is a timely and consistent leading indicator for the economy and stock market. It tends to trend downwards before a bear market and recession begins.

Figure 34

The Labor Market Conditions Index has a more useful counterpart, the Momentum Indicator. Here's FRED's definition for the Momentum Indicator.

"A positive value indicates that labor market conditions are above their long-run average, while a negative value signifies that labor market conditions are below their long-run average."

There are 2 useful ways to look at this indicator:

1. The Momentum Indicator should be less than or equal to 0 at the top of a bull market. This is a necessary but not sufficient requirement before bear markets can begin. If the Momentum Indicator is above zero, then the stock market is probably still in a bull market.
2. The Momentum Indicator should trend downwards before a bear market starts. An upwards trending Momentum Indicator is a long term bullish sign for the stock market.

Figure 35

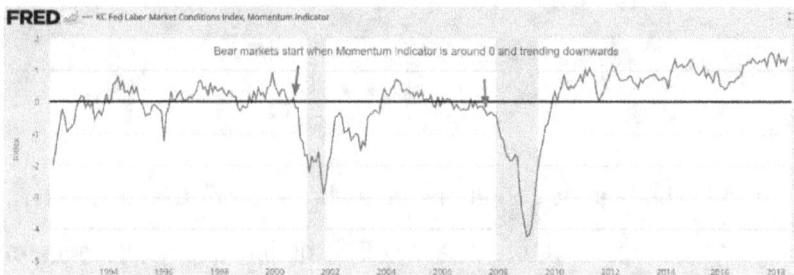

Figure 36

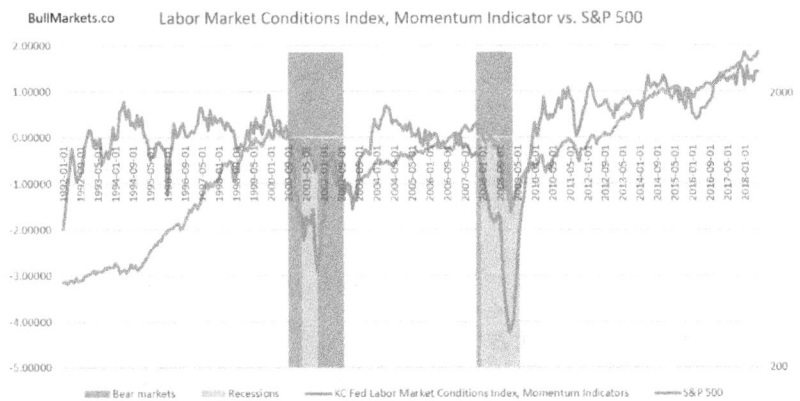

Unit Sector Profits

Unit Profits tend to peak mid-way during an economic expansion and equities bull market. This means that while Unit Profits is a CONSISTENT leading indicator, it is not a TIMELY leading indicator. It is a very early warning sign.

Figure 37

Financial conditions

Financial conditions tend to tighten before an equity bear market or economic recession begins. This is a necessary but not sufficient condition for bear markets.

Here's the Chicago Fed's National Financial Conditions Index. It is broken down into 3 subindexes.

Figure 38

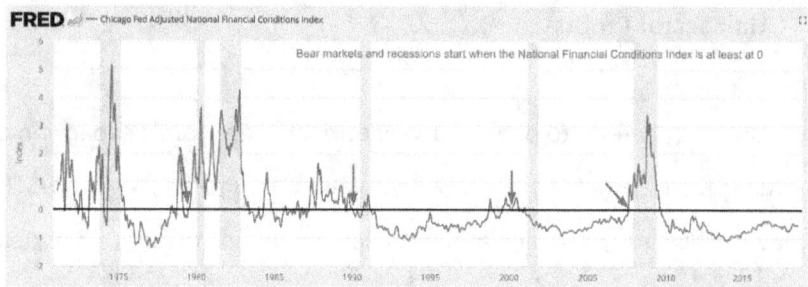

Figure 39

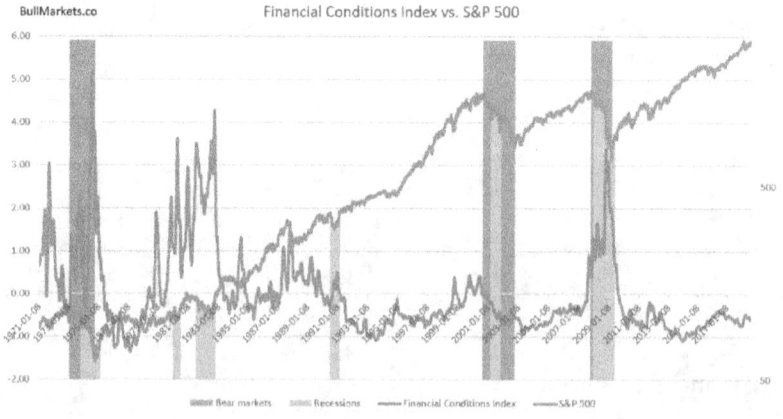

Here's the Leverage Subindex.

Figure 40

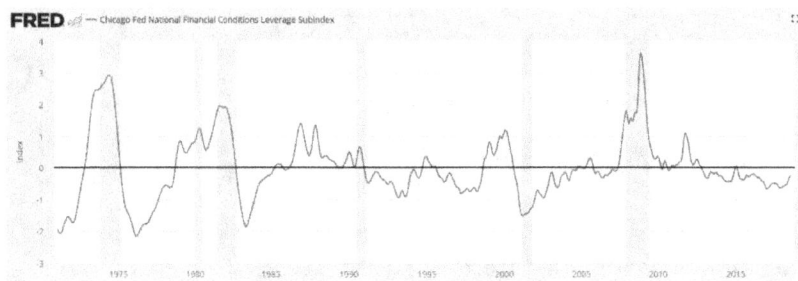

Here's the Credit Subindex.

Figure 41

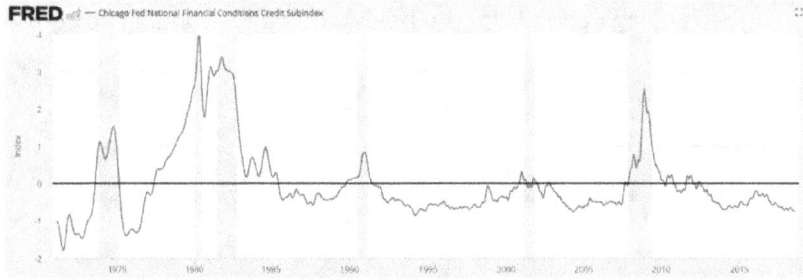

Here's the Risk Subindex.

Figure 42

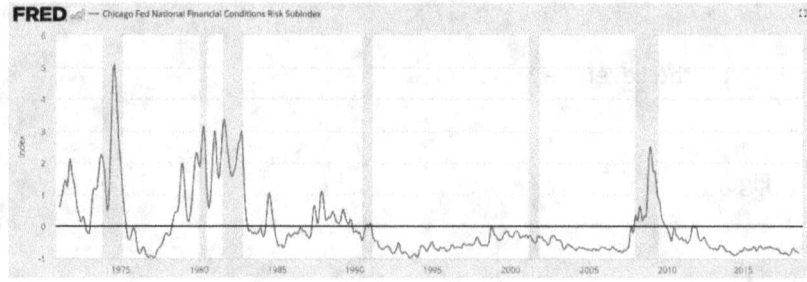

Banks' lending standards

Before a bear market starts:

1. Banks should be tightening their lending standards (figure below should be above 0%)
2. The % of banks that are tightening lending standards should be trending upwards (figure below should be trending upwards)

Figure 43

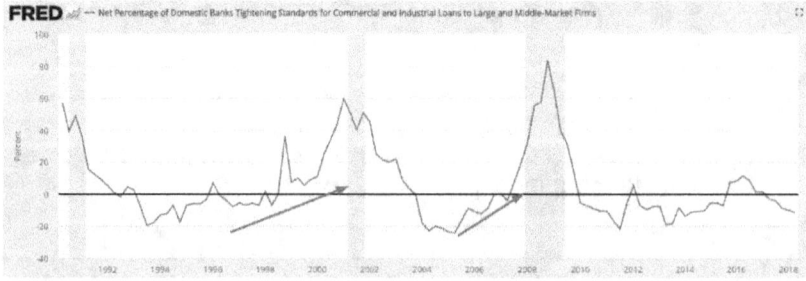

Figure 44

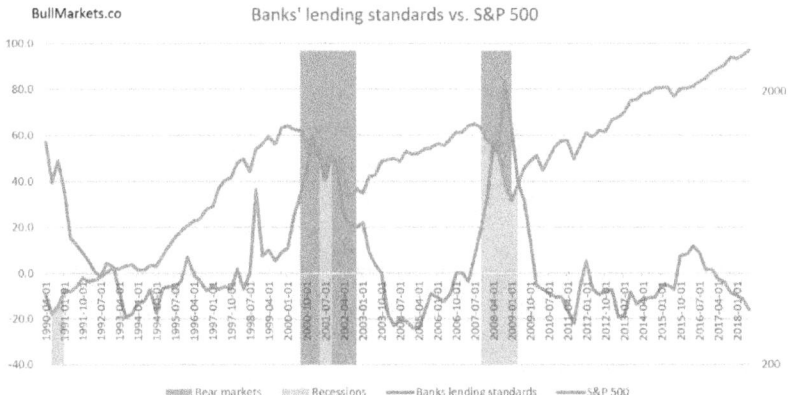

Net Earnings Revisions

Net Earnings Revisions demonstrates how many companies are increasing their forward earnings estimates minus how many companies are decreasing their forward earnings estimates. More specifically, this is the…

"Three-month moving average of the number of forward earnings estimates up less number of estimates down, expressed as a percentage of the total number of forward earnings estimates"

This figure tends to turn negative before equity bear markets and economic recessions begin. However, not all negative readings are ensued by bear markets. Hence, this is a necessary but not sufficient condition for bear markets. So if this reading is positive right now, then you know that the U.S. stock market is still in a bull market right now.

Figure 45

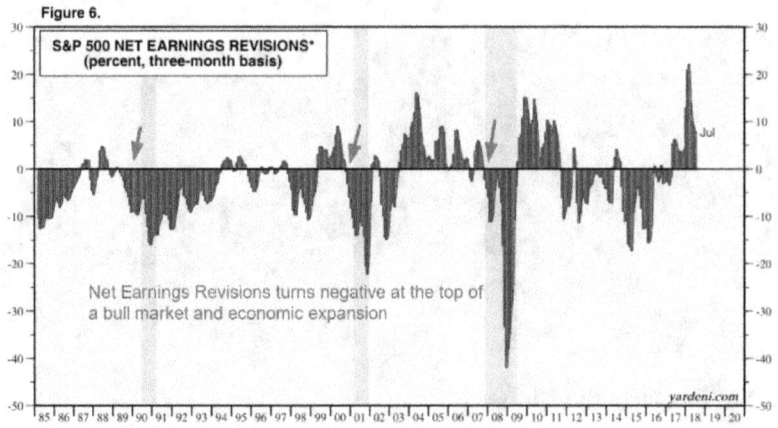

High yield spreads

Bond market investors tend to be more vigilant than stock market investors. Hence, bond market investors tend to sell high yield bonds before an equity bull market tops. This means that high yield spreads usually trend higher before an equities bull market tops.

This is a necessary but not sufficient condition for bear markets.

*Falling bond prices = higher interest rates

Figure 46

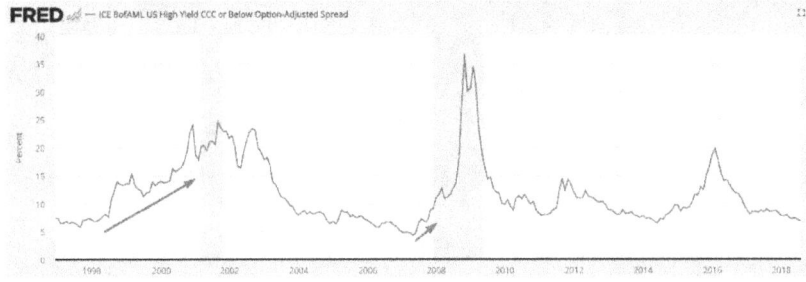

Figure 47

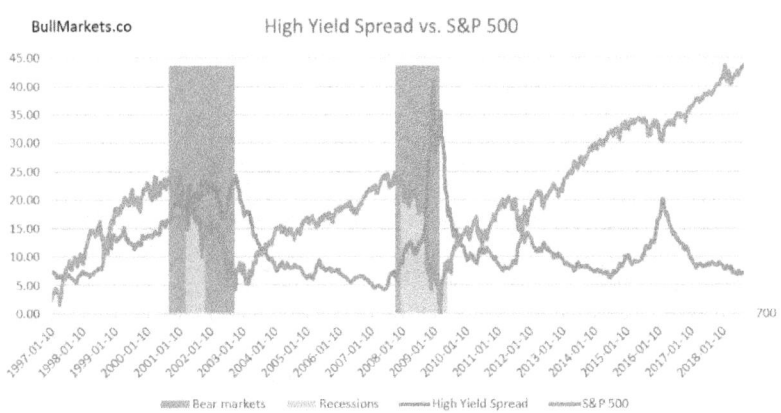

Ignore valuations

You should ignore valuations unless you're a long term investor who holds your stocks for more than 5 years. Valuations and the stock market's 1 year forward returns have a very weak correlation.

Figure 48

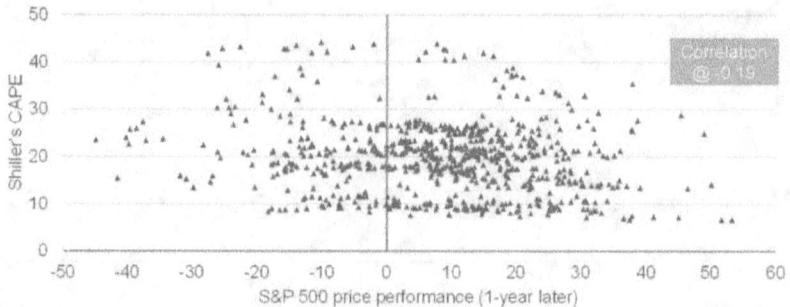

Housing

Like other big-ticket purchases, the housing sector is a leading indicator for the stock market and economy. Housing tends to peak and trend downwards before a bull market is over.

Here's Housing Starts, which looks at the number of homes being built in the U.S.

Figure 49

Figure 50

Here's New Home Sales, which looks at the number of new homes being sold in the U.S.

Figure 51

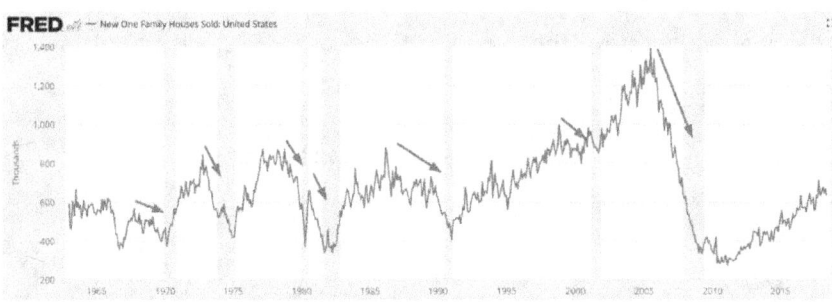

Figure 52

Real (inflation-adjusted) Retail Sales

Retail Sales looks at the dollar figure for consumer spending in the U.S. Since this is a nominal figure, it's important to adjust it for inflation.

Inflation-adjusted (real) Retail Sales tends to trend sideways (i.e. no growth) before bear markets begin. So if real Retail Sales is trending upwards right now, then you know that the U.S. stock market is still in a bull market.

Figure 53

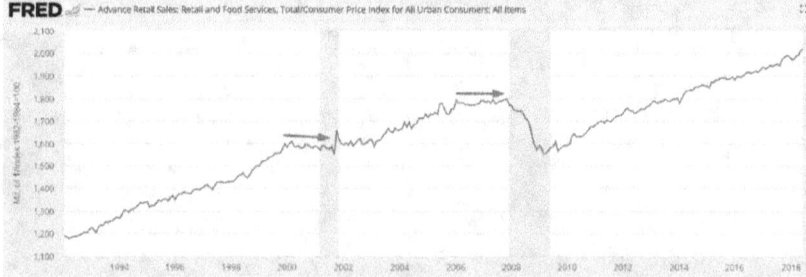

Figure 54

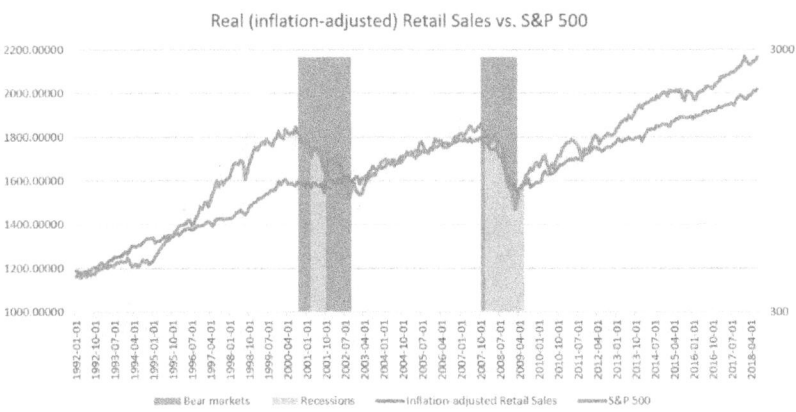

Real (inflation-adjusted) Corporate profits

Inflation-adjusted corporate profits tend to trend downwards before an equity bear market and economic recession begins. So if real corporate profits are trending higher, then the stock market is probably in a bull market right now.

Figure 55

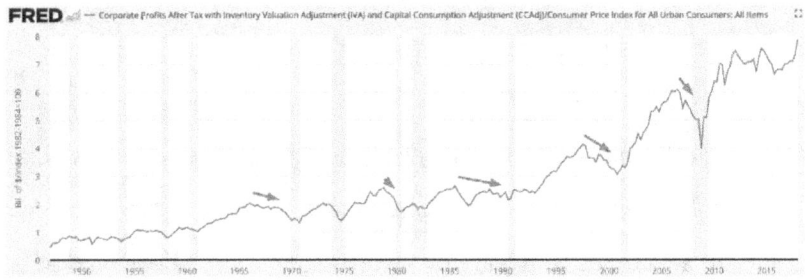

Figure 56

As you can see, these leading indicators lead the U.S. stock market and the economy. Bull markets continue until these indicators start to issue warning signs.

Out of these leading indicators, which is the best? Which leading indicator is the most timely and consistent?

Economic indicators related to big-ticket sales (e.g. auto sales, housing) tend to be too early. These indicators deteriorate long before bull markets end. That's why we don't pay too much attention to economic indicators that are related to big-ticket sales.

The best timely and consistent leading indicator is Initial Claims. Initial Claims tends to trend upwards just before an equity bear market begins. It also tends to trend downwards soon after a bear market ends.

How do we know that Initial Claims is the best timely and consistent leading indicator?

Remember: good traders don't "guess". They don't eyeball the data through the charts. Instead, good traders execute their trading strategies through quantitative trading models. We know that Initial Claims is the best leading indicator because the data proves it. Later in this book I will show you how to use Initial Claims in a trading model that generates an average of 16% per year. But first, let me show you how to create your own quantitative trading models. Trading models are based on backtesting market and economic data.

How to backtest economic indicators

As we've mentioned before, the economic data's month-to-month fluctuations don't matter. What matters is the data's **trend**. Hence, the first step in backtesting an indicator is to calculate the indicator's trend.

An easy way to calculate the economic indicator's trend is to use moving averages on the data. These moving averages smooth out random fluctuations in the data and focus on the trend. There are 2 primary ways to determine the economic data's trend through moving averages.

1. Create a moving average for the economic indicator. If the moving average is going up, then the economic indicator is deemed as "trending upwards". If the moving average is going down, then the economic indicator is deemed as "trending downwards".
2. Create a moving average for the economic indicator. If the current data is above the moving average, then the economic indicator is deemed as "trending upwards". If the current data is below the moving average, then the economic indicator is deemed as "trending downwards".

I prefer to use the second method to determine the economic indicator's trend.

So how do you know which moving average to use? This is mostly up to you. At the minimum, use a 3-number moving average (i.e. 3 week moving average for weekly economic data and 3 month moving average for monthly economic data). At the maximum, use a 12-number moving average (i.e. 12 week moving average for weekly economic data and 12 month moving average for monthly economic data).

Now we get to the time-consuming part. We need to find economic indicators that reverse approximately at the same time as the stock market makes long term reversals.

1. Create a list of the stock market's long term top and bottom dates (e.g. bull market tops and bear market bottoms).
2. Use your economic data trending method to determine BUY and SELL dates. Your BUY date = when the economic data reverses and first starts to "trend upwards". Your SELL date = when the economic data reverses and first starts to "trend downwards".

3. Compare the stock market's top and bottom dates with your economic indicator's BUY and SELL dates. The closer the stock market's top/bottom dates are with the economic indicator's BUY/SELL dates, the better the economic indicator is.

Here's how I turned Initial Claims into a quantitative trading model for the S&P 500

Initial Claims Model

As you already know, Initial Claims is a leading indicator for the economy. And since the economy and stock market move in the same direction in the long run, Initial Claims is also a leading indicator for the stock market.

Initial Claims and the S&P 500 tend to trend in the opposite direction.

Figure 57

Initial Claims vs S&P 500

This model is very simple. It has 3 lines:

1. Buy and hold SSO (S&P 500 2x leveraged ETF), UNLESS...
2. Initial Claims is above its 52 week (1 year) moving average for 8 consecutive weeks (2 months). When this happens, SELL SSO and shift to 100% cash.
3. Shift back to 100% long SSO when Initial Claims is no longer above its 1 year moving average.

This strategy yields an average of 12.55% per year from 1969 to present.

In comparison, simply buying and holding SSO from 1969 to present would yield an average annual return of 11.4%. Buying and holding SPY (S&P 500's non-leveraged ETF) during that same period would yield an average annual return of 7%.

It sounds like this strategy isn't a big improvement vs. "buy and hold". But here's the main advantage behind this model: it is less volatile than buying and holding SSO because it helps you avoid some parts of bear markets in which SSO gets clobbered.

Go to the link in brackets to download the data in Excel from the BullMarkets.co website (https://bullmarkets.co/wp-content/uploads/2018/05/initial-claims-trading-model.xlsx

Here are the model's historical BUY and SELL dates. I have included the hypothetical SSO prices.

*SSO has only existed since 2006. I calculated a hypothetical SSO by multiplying the S&P 500's daily returns by 2x.

Figure 58

Buy date	SSO Buy $	Sell date	SSO Sell $	Profit
14/7/09	11836.98	present	83281.9	604%
22/1/08	31155.54	18/3/08	31830.9	2%
24/6/03	18822.65	4/12/07	39043.09	107%
11/12/01	27480.97	8/4/03	15104.04	-45%
26/9/00	45987.03	21/11/00	40641.85	-12%
12/12/95	10114.26	29/8/00	51518.44	409%
18/6/91	3947.6	23/5/95	7408.43	88%
27/3/90	3315.43	22/5/90	3645.36	10%
28/10/86	1959.54	20/6/89	2982.98	52%
26/11/85	1406.43	23/9/86	1903.68	35%
25/6/85	1262.44	24/5/85	1244.19	-1%
8/1/85	947.66	21/5/85	1262.19	33%
23/11/82	646.55	25/9/84	970.17	50%
23/9/80	648.51	22/9/81	515.8	-20%
15/5/79	382.85	14/8/79	458.6	20%
23/1/79	403.55	20/3/79	402.1	0%
16/11/76	409.43	9/1/79	393.57	-4%
1/7/75	376.08	9/11/76	403.62	7%
9/10/73	545.14	22/1/74	413.1	-24%
21/9/71	454.48	11/9/73	479.35	5%
22/12/70	375.91	7/9/71	471.27	25%
9/9/69	414.82	4/11/69	448.94	8%

This trading model, which is purely driven by economic data, can be improved if we can eliminate some of the false SELL signals. These false SELL signals often make us sell too early and then buy back into the stock market at a higher price.

The easiest way to improve economic data-driven trading models is to add trend following components.

How to outperform with Buy and Wait. Step 3: Combine fundamental analysis with technical analysis to help you predict big declines in the stock market more accurately

You can combine trend following models with economic data to help you achieve even higher returns in the U.S. stock market.

Selling late (after the stock market peaks) is generally a better idea than selling early (before the stock market peaks). The stock market has a bullish bias because it goes up more often than it goes down. You are more likely to sell too early than to sell too late. It's better to lose a bit of money by selling after the stock market peaks than to miss out on even more profits by selling far too early. This means that it's better to be a trend follower in the stock market (turn bullish/bearish after the market reverses) than it is to be a contrarian (turn bullish/bearish before the market reverses).

This is where trend following comes in.

Trend following's basic belief is that "the price must confirm your market outlook". In other words…

1. If you turn bearish because Economic Indicator XYZ is starting to deteriorate, you should wait until the trend confirms your market outlook (i.e. the stock market starts to fall) before selling.
2. If you turn bullish because Economic Indicator XYZ is starting to improve, you should wait until the trend confirms your market outlook (i.e. the stock market starts to rise) before buying.

Moving averages are simple but effective trend following indicators. I like to use "golden crosses" and "death crosses", which are also popular trend following indicators.

1. A "golden cross" is when the market's 50 daily moving average crosses above its 200 daily moving average.
2. A "death cross" is when the market's 50 daily moving average crosses below its 200 daily moving average.

We buy and hold SSO unless Initial Claims is trending downwards in the original Initial Claims model. But this model has too many false signals. Sometimes Initial Claims trends upwards while the stock market is still going up. (All major stock market declines happen within the context of an upwards trending Initial Claims, but not all upwards trending Initial Claims lead to declines in the stock market.)

That's why we use these "golden crosses" and "death crosses" to help us eliminate some false SELL signals. Here's the new version of this model. I call it the Golden/Death Cross Model with Initial Claims Filter.

When to BUY (shift from 100% to 100% long SSO)

1. **Indicator:** Buy SSO when the S&P 500 makes a "golden cross", AND... the 50sma remains above its 200sma for 5 consecutive trading days (in other words, the S&P sustains a "golden cross" for 5 consecutive days).

Position size: 100% long SSO

When to SELL (shift from 100% long SSO to 100% cash)

Only SELL your SSO if both of these indicators occur:

1. **Indicator 1:** When the S&P 500 makes a "death cross", AND...
2. **Indicator 2:** Initial Claims is above its 52 week moving average for 8 consecutive weeks.

This is a chart of the S&P 500. Orange areas are when you should be long (based on this model).

Figure 59

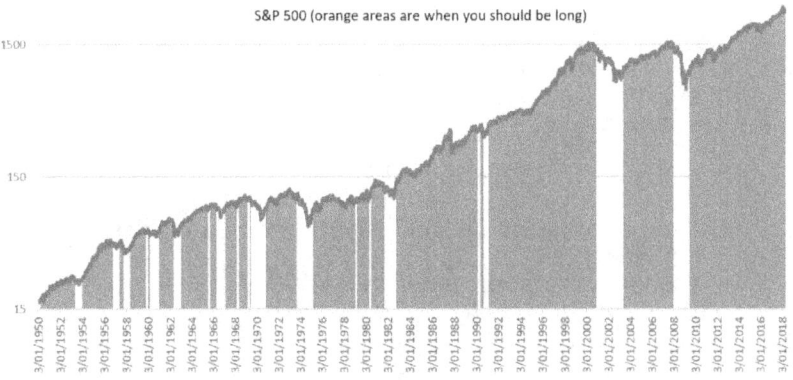

Go to the link in brackets to download the backtest and data in Excel from the BullMarkets.co website (https://bullmarkets.co/wp-content/uploads/2018/05/golden-death-cross-model-with-initial-claims-overlap.xlsx)

The logic behind this model is simple.

1. Buy and hold until the economy (the stock market's fundamentals) starts to deteriorate AND the stock market starts to trend downwards. SELL when both of these 2 things happen.
2. Buy back into the stock market when the market starts to trend upwards (i.e. makes a "golden cross")

So why don't we wait until Initial Claims starts to trend downwards (i.e. the economy improves) before buying back into the stock market? Why do we only use Initial Claims to help us determine when to sell?

That's because bear markets often bottom before the economy starts to improve.

1. The bear market of 2007-2009 bottomed in March 2009. The economic recession ended in June 2009.

2. The bear market of 1973-1974 bottomed in October 1974. The economic recession ended in March 1975.
3. The bear market of 1968 - 1970 bottomed in May 1970. The economic recession ended in November 1970.

Remember what I said before: bear market bottoms are technical in nature. The first leg of a bull market is often an oversold bounce (the stock market was too oversold in the bear market). Then the economy improves, which gives the new bull market even more upside gas.

How bear markets bottom

As I've already mentioned, the Golden/Death Cross Model with Initial Claims Filter only buys AFTER the stock market has already bottomed. It doesn't try to "catch the falling knife".

Trying to catch the falling knife in a bear market is extremely dangerous. You will lose a lot of money in the short term if the market keeps going down and you buy too early.

Remember: buying too early is the same thing as buying too late. I'd rather buy "too late" (after the market has already gone reversed upwards) when we have confirmation that the bear market is over.

There is no way to know exactly how much the stock market will fall before a bear market is over. It might be -40%, -50%, -60%, or -70%. As you can see, this is a very wide range. Bear markets are marked by widespread fear, which means that the market might fall by more than you initially thought.

Instead of trying to catch the falling knife and guess when the stock market will bottom, you should wait until the market tells you that the bottom is already in.

So how do you know if the bear market is definitely already over? Simple. Just wait for a "golden cross" (the S&P's 50 daily moving average crosses above its 200 daily moving average). In the 4 historical bear markets since 1950, a "golden cross" always occurred after the bear market ended. The S&P never made a "golden cross" when it was still in a bear market.

Here is the 2007-2009 bear market. Notice how the S&P 500 didn't make a Golden Cross until the bear market was already over. It **confirmed** the bear market's bottom.

Figure 60

Here is the 2000-2002 bear market. Notice how the S&P 500 didn't make a Golden Cross until the bear market was already over. It **confirmed** the bear market's bottom.

Figure 61

Here is the 1973-1974 bear market. Notice how the S&P 500 didn't make a Golden Cross until the bear market was already over. It **confirmed** the bear market's bottom.

Figure 62

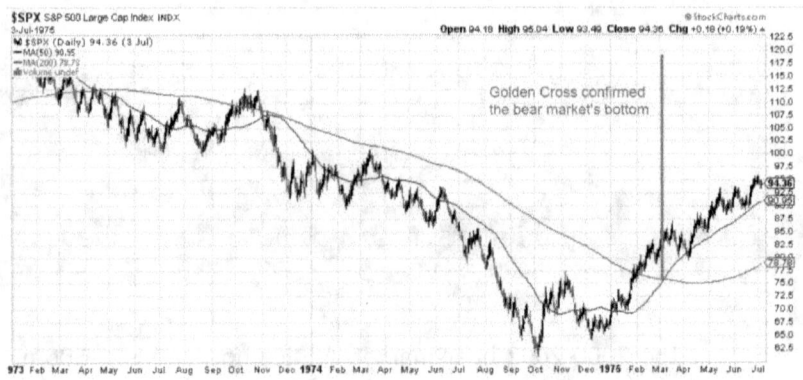

Here is the 1968-1970 bear market. Notice how the S&P 500 didn't make a Golden Cross until the bear market was already over. It **confirmed** the bear market's bottom.

Figure 63

This is the 2007-2009 bear market. Notice how the Golden Cross didn't occur until the bear market was already over. It **confirmed** the bear market's bottom.

Figure 64

This is the 2000-2002 bear market. Notice how the Golden Cross confirmed the bear market's bottom.

Figure 65

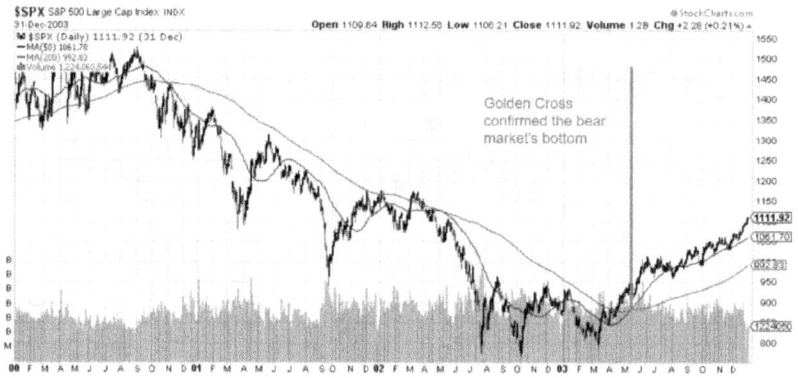

This is the 1973-1974 bear market. Notice how the Golden Cross occurred AFTER the S&P 500's bear market was already over.

Figure 66

This is the 1968-1970 bear market. Notice how the Golden Cross occurred AFTER the bear market was already over.

Figure 67

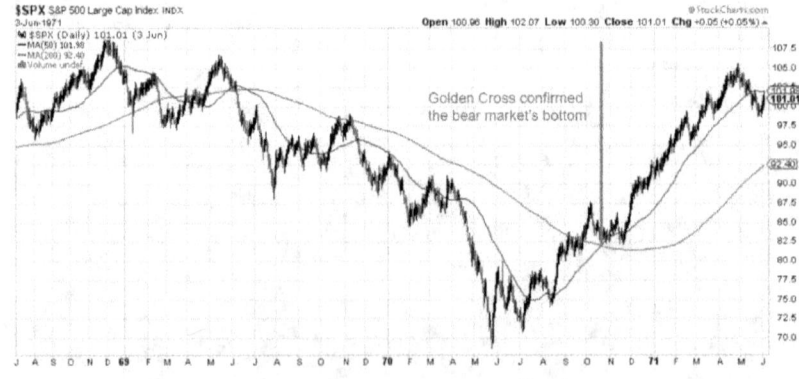

Does Buy and Wait apply to other countries' stock markets?

Can you use economic data to trade other countries' stock markets in a way that lets you significantly beat buy and hold? Or does this trading strategy only apply to the U.S. stock market?

Here are the data and facts. You can use economic data to consistently and profitably trade other countries' stock markets if:

1. The country is a developed nation.
2. The country has reliable economic data. For example, China does not have reliable economic data. Some of its data is fabricated by the government.

Here's an example. Canadian traders who use this model will consistently outperform those who buy and hold the Canadian stock market in the long run. This model has 2 lines:

1. Buy and hold a Canadian stock market (TSX) ETF **UNLESS**
2. Canada's Unemployment Rate exceeds its 10 month moving average AND the TSX falls below its 10 month moving average at the same time.

The Canadian stock market yielded an average annual return of 5.42% from 1980 – present. This trading strategy yields an average annual return of 7.09% from 1980 – present. If you use a leveraged ETF for the Canadian stock market with this trading strategy, your average annual returns will be even higher.

Here is when this model states that you should be long the TSX (Canadian stock market). Be long during the orange shaded eras.

Figure 68

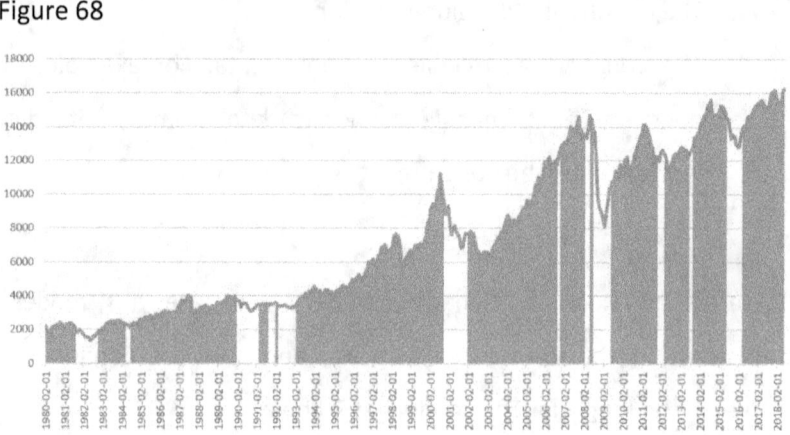

Go to the link in brackets to download the data and backtest in Excel from the BullMarkets.co website (https://bullmarkets.co/wp-content/uploads/2018/08/canada-stock-market-model.xlsx)

Why non-Americans need to care about the U.S. stock market

Every stock market investor and trader must understand and be able to predict what happens next to the U.S. stock market, regardless of which country's stock market they trade. This is because the U.S. stock market impacts **every other stock market in the world**. When the U.S. stock market makes a big decline, every other stock market in the world makes a big decline.

For example, the U.S. stock market was in a bear market from 2007-2009. Every single stock market in the world fell (e.g. German, Indian, Chinese, Australian, Canadian, South African, Brazilian). This is because although the U.S. only accounts for 25% of world GDP, it accounts for 50% of the world's financial markets. The U.S. stock market and financial markets are massive. When the elephant in the room moves, it impacts everybody and everything else in the room.

Closing Remarks

Beating buy and hold significantly in the long run isn't hard. In order to do so, you must:

1. Focus on fact-based (data-driven) analysis instead of faith-based (dogma-driven) analysis.
2. Focus on sensible trading instead of the sensational headlines that financial media promotes.
3. Combine fundamental analysis (economic data) with technical analysis.

And for the record, most finance professionals can't even beat buy and hold in the long run. That's because a lot of conventional trading "wisdom" and many conventional trading strategies are wrong or ineffective.

One of the simplest ways to significantly beat buy and hold in the long run is a trading strategy I call "Buy and Wait". Buy and Wait has 3 steps:

1. Buy leveraged ETFs. The problem with leveraged ETFs is that they decay (erode) and lose a lot of value during bear markets.
2. Use fundamentals to help you avoid a big chunk of bear markets.

3. Combine technical analysis with fundamental analysis to give you more accurate BUY and SELL signals for bull markets and bear markets.

In other words, you BUY, hold, and wait until you should SELL. Avoid big declines in the stock market.

I would like to leave you with one last piece of advice.

Never trust someone else's word when trading or investing. Always look at the data and facts for yourself.

Cheers,
Troy Bombardia
BullMarkets.co

If you want a free quantitative trading model that yields an average annual return of 17.2%, please go to https://bullmarkets.co and sign up for my stock market outlook newsletter.

www.ingramcontent.com/pod-product-compliance
Lightning Source LLC
Chambersburg PA
CBHW052329220526
45472CB00001B/335